CAREER PATTERNS IN EDUCATION

CAREER PATTERNS IN EDUCATION

Women, Men and Minorities in
Public School Administration

Flora Ida Ortiz
University of California, Riverside

PRAEGER SPECIAL STUDIES • PRAEGER SCIENTIFIC
A J.F. BERGIN PUBLISHERS BOOK

Library of Congress Cataloging in Publication Data

Ortiz, Flora Ida.
 Career patterns in education.

 A J.F. Bergin Publishers book.
 Bibliography: p.
 Includes index.
 1. School administrators—United States.
 I. Title
 LB2831.62.O77   371.2'01'02373   80-29490
                                         AACR2

Published in 1982 by Praeger Publishers
CBS Educational and Professional Publishing
A Division of CBS, Inc.
521 Fifth Avenue, New York, New York 10175

0123456789   056   987654321

Printed in the United States of America

CONTENTS

To the memory of Leo R. Ortiz
(1906–1980)

ACKNOWLEDGMENTS

A number of persons contributed to the present work. My main intellectual debt is to Laurence Iannaccone. His work and that of his students served as the springboard for the present work. Additionally, Professor Iannaccone provided invaluable aid during the development of the theoretical framework.

I am grateful to colleagues who have saved me from many errors: to Ralph Bradshaw and Martin Burlingame, who read and commented on the first four chapters of the work, and to Carlos Cortes, who provided support and advice throughout the preparation of the manuscript.

I also wish to acknowledge the cooperation and support I received from those persons involved in this study. Without them this work would not have been possible.

CHAPTER 1

Introduction

One of the most pervasive social arguments has been the concern over the lack of understanding social behavior to the degree that effective policy decisions can be made. The irrelevancy of social science research to social problems has been critical to this argument. On the one hand, reformers are impatient with social problems and demand quick remedies. While others claim not enough is known to act in a meaningful way. An area of special concern in this regard is the integration and participation of women and minorities in occupational and organizational settings.

The present book attempts to show how social science theories, socialization and role, do provide a means for understanding occupational and organizational participation. Moreover, a way to predict the eventual careers which can be established due to organizational characteristics and personal attributes is presented. Therefore, a primary purpose of this report is to show how social science research can be utilized by policy makers in their decision-making processes.

Educational administration is used as the case in point to show how socialization and role theories help to explain the participation of its members. This report does not show surprising findings. In fact, the critical characteristic of the present study is how faithfully the prevalent socialization and role theories are verified.

The analysis which is being presented in this report is based on data collected from 350 school administrators. Administrators were defined as those who were occupying school positions which required the California State administrative credential.

Adult socialization has been dealt with more thoroughly through the study of professionalization (Becker, 1952; 1962; 1956; Merton, 1960; Caplow, 1954; Hughes, 1958) and organizational socialization. For example, Becker and Carper (1956), Schein (1968; 1961; 1971), Presthus (1962), Whyte (1956), Corwin (1965), Glaser (1964), and others have reported on organizational settings. Other researchers have presented explanations regarding adult behavior in educational institutions. For example, Lewis (1975), Cohen and March (1974), and others report on university participation. Those researchers who have studied public schools have reported on teachers (Dreeben, 1973; Lortie, 1975; Becker, 1952; Waller, 1933; Griffiths, 1965), elementary principals (Bridges, 1965; Mascaro, 1973; McCabe, 1972; Wiggins, 1970; Wolcott, 1973; Gross and Trask, 1976), and

1

superintendents (Carlson, 1961; 1962; 1972; Griffiths, 1966; Gross, et al., 1958; Halpin, 1950; Seeman, 1960).

Those investigations dealing with teachers (Griffiths, 1965; Becker, 1952; Lortie, 1975; Waller, 1933) have delineated certain types and have reported on the consequences to the profession. The reports dealing with elementary principals (Bridges, 1965; McCabe, 1972; Mascaro, 1973; Gross and Trask, 1976) indicate the principals tend to increase their bureaucratic role over time. The role studied most extensively as a career has been that of the superintendent (AASA, 1960; Knezevitch, 1975; Carlson, 1962; 1971; 1972). The studies indicate a lengthy process of training and experience. Other studies indicate organizational press and personal adjustment (Gross, et al., 1958; Carlson, 1961; 1962; 1972).

Studies which have looked at the various professional roles found in public school organizations are not widely reported. For example, positions other than the teacher, principal, and superintendent have not received extensive study. Also, studies dealing with the quality of the participation of women and minorities have not been very numerous.

To fill this gap the present work is an attempt to specify selected adult socialization processes in public school institutions. The focus is on those processes which determine upward mobility within the school hierarchy. Organizational factors and individual or personal attributes which contribute to the processes will be identified. Lastly, the quality of organizational participation will be examined.

Socialization processes are defined as those changes which occur in persons as they participate in organizational settings. The underlying assumption is that being a member of an organization, engaging in the organizational activities, and fulfilling organizational expectations requires fundamental and continuing personal changes. The present study attempts to show how some of these changes occur, with a primary focus on those who are engaged in advancing within the school bureaucracy. It will also be shown that presently existing social science explanations are useful in predicting career patterns.

FOCUS OF THE PRESENT STUDY

In the present study, socialization processes are examined as they apply to individuals establishing careers in public school institutions. The hierarchical structure consists of students (clients), teachers, principals, central office personnel, and superintendent. Because the focus of this study is on the internal structure of the organization and those individuals who establish careers within it, students (the clients) and the school board are not included. Also, because this study is primarily concerned with those whose participation is directly related to the goals of the organization (instruction, teaching and learning), organizational participants such as custodians, secretaries, nurses, and cafeteria personnel are not included.

In brief, the socialization processes which are examined are those which impact upon teachers, principals, central office administrators, and superintendents. Because this study is concerned with socialization processes as they affect the mobility of individuals, the primary focus is on school administrators.

THEORETICAL FRAMEWORK

The two dimensions that are involved in the process of organizational socialization are organizational factors and personal attributes. Organizational factors are structural and conceptualized as hierarchy (Weber, 1969), as organizational space (Katz and Kahn, 1977), and as deposits of opportunity and power (Kanter, 1977).

The hierarchical concept denotes differences due to rank and level. The organizational space concept denotes differences in organizational position regarding working environment, and opportunities to engage in meaningful activities. The deposits of opportunity and power (Kanter, 1977) concept denotes differences in degree of opportunity and power which are present in organizational positions. Personal attributes such as age, sex, social class, and ethnic origin, are ascribed and other characteristics such as training, experience, knowledge, skills, and attitudes are achieved.

Within the organization certain structural organizational factors interact as individuals gain access to the organization, acquire membership, advance, and finally establish an organizational career. The interaction between the factors is differential in relation to the personal attributes. Access to an organization is gained when role identity and organizational need are complimentary. That is, tentative acceptance of the individual is granted by the organization when an individual convincingly displays his/her possession of the requisite knowledge, skills, intentions, commitments, and loyalties to it. For example, a teacher is hired into the school district with tenure to be granted after three successful years of participation. Membership is acquired when the organization's members' perceptions of the organizational position and the person's ascribed and achieved attributes are congruent. For example, a woman holding a teacher's position is viewed as proper by the organization because the organizational position requires those characteristics ascribed to women. Providing services and engaging in interaction with children rather than adults (Hughes, 1958; Caplow, 1954) is viewed as especially appropriate for women.

The internal structure of the organization is composed of organizational spaces (Katz and Kahn, 1966). These spaces are differentiated in three ways (Ortiz, 1972): 1) the working environment, 2) interpersonal relationships, and 3) professional activities. The working environment may be evaluated in terms of its physical characteristics: 1) central and visible location, 2) cleanliness and pleasantness, 3) proximity to the organizational leaders, and 4) quality of furnishings and office equipment.

Organizational spaces provide differentially for opportunities to develop intensive and extensive interpersonal relationships. This characteristic is dependent, in part, on the working environment described above. Intensive interpersonal relationships are measured in terms of frequency and duration of interaction. Extensive interpersonal relationships are measured in terms of quantity and variety of relationships. Establishment of intensive interpersonal relationships with immediate superiors and peers is requisite for successful membership. Establishment of extensive interpersonal relationships with subordinates and more distant superiors is likewise necessary for successful incorporation in the organization.

Organizational spaces also provide the occupant with differential opportunities to engage in professional activities. Professional activities are defined as those which are directly related to the organization's "mission", e.g., meeting with the school board to approve personnel procedures or presenting a research report to the professional association at the annual convention. The continuous and increasing participation in such activities insures membership and increases the likelihood of mobility within the organization.

Kanter (1977) claims organizational positions contain differing degrees of opportunity and power. Opportunity is defined as "a more dynamic concept in which it is the relationship of a present position to a larger structure and to anticipated future positions that is critical" (161). This is to say that positions are important in relation to others, and they must contain the promise of upward movement.

Opportunity positions are characterized in the following ways: the positions provide for more frequent career reviews than others; they maximize the exposure of the position holder; position holders engage in project assignments to task groups with more senior people; "two hats" may be required, e.g., more connections and knowledge of more than one function are necessary (Kanter, 1977:133). Positions which are restrictive in any of the above ways are limited in the opportunities that they can provide for the individuals occupying them.

Power is defined as the "ability to get things done, to mobilize resources, to get and use whatever it is that a person needs for the goals he or she is attempting to meet" (166). Power positions provide informal political influence, access to resources, outside status, and sponsorship and mobility prospects. Organizational activities which route individuals to power are: 1) those which are extraordinary, such as new ventures or pulling off risks; 2) those which are visible such as reorganization, and 3) those which are relevant (176-181).

Power may also be acquired through others. Kanter states, "In a large complex system, it is almost a necessity for power to come from social connections, especially those outside of the immediate work group. Such connections need to be long-term and stable and include sponsors, peers, and subordinates" (181). Power is that force which is the most desired within an organizational setting.

Individuals wishing to establish organizational careers assume power will be acquired.

Mobility requires movement along three dimensions (Schein, 1971). Movement may be vertical, i.e., one's rank or level in the organization is increased or decreased (Schein, 1971:403). For example, a teacher becomes a department head. The change means that the individual has acquired a new title and position, additional salary, and authority in relation to the other teachers. The reverse could also occur with the loss of the three characteristics mentioned above.

Movement may be circumferential, i.e., one's function or division of the organization is changed (403). For example, a teacher becomes a principal. The change has not only meant a new position and title, additional compensation and authority, but the individual has also departed from instructing children to administering and managing adults. The reverse could also occur. In many cases, movement may be both vertical or circumferential such as in the example presented above.

Movement may also be radial, i.e., one's centrality in the organization is increased or decreased (403). Centrality refers to closeness to the organizational leaders; in schools it would be to superintendents and school board members. For example, a principal is nominated to represent the other principals in the executive committee. This change denotes a difference between the nominee and the other principals. But most important, it shows that this principal will be engaged in activities related to the complete school district. This participation will mean increased interaction with school officials and an opportunity to obtain information not readily accessible to other principals and those hierarchically below the principalship position.

Corresponding to these three types of movement, three types of boundaries characterize the internal structure of the organization. The hierarchical boundaries separate the hierarchical levels from one another (Schein, 1971; 404-405). These boundaries are usually in the form of formal requirements such as degrees, credentials, certificates, and varied experiences. The functional or the departmental boundaries separate departments, divisions, or different functional groupings from one another. In school administraton, these boundaries separate areas such as the elementary from the secondary principalship, or finance from personnel posts. The inclusion boundaries separate individuals or groups who differ in the degree of their centrality. These boundaries may be intangible and necessitate informal requirements. Crossing this boundary is the most difficult process in career establishment.

The socialization processes are the result of the organizations' efforts to insure that the organizations remain hierarchically structured, with differentiated organizational spaces, limited positions providing opportunity for upward mobility, and a few restricted positions containing power. For example, a person desiring to be a superintendent will be subjected to increasing demands as he or she moves up the hierarchy; in many cases these demands are awarded by his counterparts.

SCHOOL ADMINISTRATION CAREER PATTERNS

Even though some important studies have been conducted regarding school administrators' careers (Carlson, 1961; 1962; 1972; Knezevitch, 1975; AASA, 1960), there has been a hesitancy to examine how these careers have been established. For example, Carlson's work based on secondary analyses from various sources describes the types of superintendents school districts tend to hire. The Profile of the School Superintendent (1960) reports two major career patterns of superintendents. The most common reported in districts of 100,000 or more population was teacher/principal/central office administrator/superintendent. The most common career pattern for superintendents located in smaller communities tended to be teacher/principal/ superintendent. Knezevitch's report using more recent date, 1969-70, is limited to presenting the charateristics of superintendents. Studies reporting the processes by which individuals attain administrative positions have not been reported.

As stated earlier, the two major career patterns found among superintendents were teacher/principal/superintendent and teacher/principal/central office administrator/superintendent. The first pattern was found in small communities and develops in small school districts. The second pattern is most common in larger communities with complex school district organization.

This study reports on those socialization processes present in larger organizations. Such school districts are defined as those which contain a central office. Therefore, this study looks at administrative careers which are likely to include central office experience if the superintendency is sought. The internal structure which is examined includes the hierarchical positions of teacher/principal/central office/and superintendent. The barriers are to be found between each of these positions. Each position is viewed in terms of its organizational space characteristics, its degree of power and opportunity, and its mobility features of hierarchy, functions, and centrality.

CHAPTER 2

Becoming
An Administrator

School administrators begin their school organization careers by teaching. Males teach 5-7 years and females 15 years before assuming their first administrative position (Gross and Trask, 1976). There are several reasons why males obtain administrative positions at an earlier period than do females. First, white males are strongly encouraged as teachers to become school administrators. Second, they find themselves outnumbered by women in teaching, particularly in elementary schools. Third, the strongest indicator of success in school organizations is the acquisition of an administrative position. The pervading norm that white males be successful aids in the acquisition of an administrative position.

Once an individual acquires an administrative position, the assumption is that the individual has departed from teaching and a career in administration is likely. Desire to move back to the classroom is nostalgically expressed by many administrators, but practically it is viewed as an organizational demotion and most administrators do not willingly return to the classroom.

From the data being presently reported, a general finding is that white males are more likely to occupy the vice-principalship, elementary principalship, secondary principalship, selected central office positions, the assistant, deputy, and/or associate superintendency and superintendency. Therefore, as noted in other studies (AASA, 1960), the data for this study indicate that the critical positions in the structure leading to the superintendency are those just presented.

THE VICE-PRINCIPAL

In medium sized to large school districts, the vice-principal is an important administrative entry level position. The vice-principalship tends to be a position to "try out" administrators. The administrative credential is not mandatory, and most listings of school administrators omit vice-principals. For example, as presented on Table 1, out of the 158 white males who occupy the positions presented above, 100 of them held the vice-principalship for a period of time. Out of these 100, the position was occupied by 70 of them prior to their acquisition of the administrative credential. Thus, the vice-principalship is not normally considered a legitimate administrative position. It is an important organizational position, however, because it does provide a means of departing from teaching in a gradual way.

TABLE 1. White Male School Administrators Occupying the Vice-Principalship as Part of Their Administrative Careers

Total Number of Administrators	Vice-principals	Without Credential
38 elementary principals	15	9
17 mid-high principals	11	7
29 high school principals	22	11
20 assistant superintendents	15	9
15 associate superintendents	10	9
22 deputy superintendents	15	13
17 superintendents	12	12
158	100	70

Hierarchy

A way to analyze this position is to look at it in terms of the theoretical framework which was presented earlier. One of the concepts dealing with structural organizational factors is hierarchy. The vice-principalship position is above that of the teachers and also below the principal, so that its organizational placement is hierarchically between the teacher and principal.

Organizational Space

Working Environment

In terms of its organizational space within the organization, we can look at the working environment. The most pronounced change between the teacher's working environment and that of the vice-principal is the acquisition of a private office and the relinquishment of a classroom. Another change is in the probable location of his working area. The vice-principal is more likely to be closer to the principal. Therefore, the vice-principal's working environment would be different and in most cases judged to be improved in terms of increasing privacy and proximity to superiors.

Interpersonal Relationships

In looking at the changes in interpersonal relationships, the vice-principal now has an opportunity to interact with students and teachers from throughout the school. Formerly, being confined to his classroom and most likely to level and/or subject area teachers (Charters, 1964), now he has access to everyone on the campus. Therefore, the opportunities for developing extensive interpersonal relationships have been greatly enhanced. Furthermore, being physically located closer to the principal and being his assistant now provides him with the opportunity to develop intensive interpersonal relationships with his superior. This increases the likelihood that he will also be in contact with other school administrators. The position of vice-principalship, then, does change the degree of intensive and extensive interpersonal relationships.

Activities

Another change concerns the kinds of activities in which the person is engaged. As vice-principal, the individual first of all helps the principal make decisions regarding the school. This is a change from making decisions regarding instruction in his/her classroom. The change is for a broader and more general area. Three basic distinctions can be made. The vice-principal has increased his area of function from the classroom to the school. Also, the function itself has increased from that dealing solely with instruction to that dealing with school administration and management. Third, the vice-principal is working closely with another adult, the principal. As a teacher, he/she tended to work alone with students. Decisions were personally made without much consultation or discussion (Lortie, 1968; 1975). As a vice-principal he/she is usually obligated to discuss, consult, and finally reach consensus on school decisions. The development of this relationship is important. This opportunity also avails the candidate opportunities to develop important interpersonal skills. Therefore, the position of the vice-principal provides these opportunities without committing the organization or the individual to an administrative career.

Opportunity

As we stated earlier, the vice-principalship is not a permanent administrative position. An administrative credential is not mandatory and the position may terminate at the principal's pleasure. For example, vice-principals state, "When I was asked to be vice-principal I was told right out, 'This assignment is dependent on how well you do and how well we work together.'" Another vice-principal said, "Other administrators remind me that this position is dependent on what the principal thinks of the way I get along." All of these factors contribute to the likelihood that even though vertical and functional movement occurred at the time the position was assumed, radial movement or movement towards the center is not possible. It therefore means that the position of the vice-principal is a "stepping-stone," a "grooming," or an interim position. It is not likely that a career can be established on this position.

Nevertheless, the vice-principal's position contains a critical degree of opportunity. It is a position which can mean the difference between an administrative or teaching career. The "opportunity" exists because it places the individual alongside the principal; it affords the individual expanded and different experiences; and it places the person where he may display publicly his skills, attitudes and knowledge. Its temporariness is a positive characteristic in that the individual must leave the position, so the chances of assuming the principalship are increased.

THE PRINCIPAL

Movement from the vice-principalship is inevitable. For those who advance, the most likely position which is assumed is the principalship. In order to obtain the principal's position, it is necessary to have an administrator's credential. In most states, one of the requirements for the administrative credential is 3-5 years of teaching experience. Most principals have taught at least five years. The principal's position holds permanency. As we stated earlier, it is possible for a person to hold a principal's position for the duration of an administrative career. The elementary principalship is particularly prone to this kind of permanence (Gross and Trask, 1976; Covel, 1977; Wolcott, 1973:207).

The elementary, the junior or middle school, and the high school principalships are the three line administrative positions at the building level. The elementary principalship may be assumed by teachers from any level, content area, or area of specialization. High school teaching experience, and/or high school vice-principalship experience is of greater importance in secondary principalship positions. Data collected in the present study show similar findings as reported by Hempill, et al., (1965). They write:

> Most senior high school principals have an extensive teaching background. ...The survey indicates that 60 percent of the principals have between four and fourteen years (experience). Generally, this experience has been either in the natural sciences or mathematics, social science, and to some extent in the fields of English or speech. Approximately one-third of the principals have taught either mathematics or natural science in secondary schools.

> More than half report at least one year of experience as an athletic coach or director. Likewise, about half of the principals report at least one year's experience in

counseling or guidance work. Approximately, one-third have been elementary school principals, and many have had experience as elementary school teachers. The most frequently traversed route to the senior high school principalship is through secondary school teaching (5)

Hierarchy

The principalship positions differ from each other in terms of their hierarchical placement, the character of their internal organizational space, and the degree to which they contain opportunity and power. Each difference will now be presented.

The elementary principalship is the lowest line administrative position in the hierarchy of school administration. Elementary schools are the most numerous, are predominantly staffed by women, and the clients are very young children. Their clients are drawn from a single and smaller area (unless integration efforts require otherwise) which contributes to a more limiting position. Consistent with the present data reported upon, Wolcott (1973) also indicated in his study that persons holding the elementary principalship are those interested in staying there. He states:

In the principalship, at least among Ed's colleagues, career commitment was generally taken to mean a commitment to the position of elementary school principal and to one's school district as well.

Their stated objective in this regard was a consideration for the long-range interests of the district, rather than in the preservation of the status quo in their own group. As one principal explained: "I would have ranked one candidate higher, but I think of the elementary principalship as a career. He's a stronger candidate than some of the others, but I just don't think he's going to stay - he'll stay about four or five years and use us as a stepping stone" (207-209).

In contrast, high school principals express a different attitude which is also similar to what Hemphill, et. al. (1965) found. They state:

Despite general satisfaction with educational administration as a career choice, most secondary principals are not satisfied to remain in their present position. Only about one-quarter indicated that they had no desire to move to another position. Many aspire to the superintendency, while others would move to a principalship in a larger school (10).

In summary, it can be reported that the elementary and

secondary principalships differ in their hierarchical placement and in their degree of permanency.

Organizational Space

Working Environment

The elementary principalship, then, is expected to possess some of those characteristics found in other lower hierarchy positions. The working environment is more confined than that of the other principalships. For example, the secondary principals' geographical area is greater and more extensive, and enrollment is usually larger. Likewise, the office area is larger and more complex. Elementary school administrative units tend to consist of the principal's office, the secretary's desk, counter area, a work room for the teachers and, maybe, an extra room for personnel such as school nurses. In contrast, secondary schools tend to have more expanded services, where vice-principals, school counselors, additional secretarial help and numerous offices for storage and extra services are included. High schools are the most complex. The principal's office may consist of his office, two vice-principals (data in the present study show two cases of boys' and girls' vice-principals), counselors, extra-curricular support staff, special services staff, and various clerical services staff. In brief, the organizations that principals head differ in complexity, and the elementary principalship is the smallest and least complex.

Interpersonal Relationships

Principals do not have a clearly identified superior. Directors, specialists, coordinators, and associate superintendents of either elementary or secondary content areas may serve as supervisors. But, it is not likely that a single person is responsible for all elementary and secondary principals. The structure is such that elementary and secondary curriculum experts, assistant or associate superintendents evaluate principals. Principals, in turn, find themselves fragmented among them, but most seriously, far apart from the superintendent. This structure mitigates against the establishment of intensive relationships with superiors.

There is another problem associated with the development of intensive interpersonal relationships. That is that the principals and their superiors are in different areas of the school district. Principals rarely see their superiors. The result is that principals have to seek ways to interact with them. Additionally, they must establish patterns of interaction in order to retain and develop relationships. Elementary and secondary principals differ in the degree to which they can find means for increased interaction.

In school districts, the number of elementary principals exceeds that of any other type of principal. This could be a source of power among them, but this fact also contributes to other consequences. Because there are so many elementary principals, it is problematic for the superintendent to know them all in order to develop intensive relationships. Therefore, for a given elementary principal, it is more difficult to gain and retain the attention of the superintendent. This is equally true with all other central office officials. Other researchers report similar observations. For example, Wolcott (1973) writes:

> I have no record of (Ed Bell, the elementary principal), calling the superintendent or of the superintendent calling him, although calls were sometimes exchanged between Taft School and the superintendent's office (i.e., his secretary) concerning the preparation of reports requested specifically by the superintendent (210).

The consequence of minimal interaction with the school district's leader is the development of certain perceptions about the superintendent. An elementary principal stated, "Do those administrators really make decisions? The superintendent always seems to be studying, surveying, or working on an issue." Wolcott similarly quotes a principal saying, "I never have worked with a superintendent who really understands the role of the elementary school principal" (223). Not being personally able to gain access to the superintendent and other school leaders, principals resort to other means.

District meetings are one way to establish contact. A variety of official meetings take place during the course of the school year. Principals' meetings are one of the most common. These meetings are usually scheduled so the elementary and secondary principals may meet separately or together. Data collected from this study indicate that the most usual pattern is to have elementary principals meet early in the morning with the others meeting later. The consequence of this schedule is that those who meet later have the opportunity to go out to lunch after the meeting while the elementary principals depart to their schools. Since the leaders of the school district are readily accessible, it is likely that secondary principals are able to interact with them under informal conditions.

Membership to various school district committees would also provide a means for the development of extensive interpersonal relationships. Because of the great number of elementary principals, the likelihood of a particular elementary principal being selected is lessened. High school principals, on the other hand, are likely to hold a position in almost all district-wide committees. This activity contributes to the acquisition of additional district-wide information. Elementary principals without this asset are further inhibited in their ability to develop extensive and intensive interpersonal relationships.

Meetings also serve other functions which accentuate the differences between elementary and secondary principals. For example, meetings were important events in which administrators attempted to display their skills and knowledge. Wolcott (1973:122) similarly describes the function of meetings in the following way:

The latent functions of meetings, especially those within the educator subculture, accomplished rather different purposes. First, they served to validate role - to give visible evidence of being engaged with the "problems and issues" of schooling. Secondly, and more importantly, they served to validate existing status hierarchies and to provide a continuing process for reviewing each person's position in those hierarchies. What actually transpired at any of the meetings was never as important as the underlying issue of who could call a meeting for what purposes, who felt obligated to attend, and what kind or priority was adequate for an excuse.

Since elementary principals are at the lowest level of the hierarchy, it is not surprising to find that their attitudes towards meetings are less than favorable. Wolcott's (1973) report expresses similar elementary principals' feelings toward these meetings:

Indeed, the meeting attended by the fewest persons among Ed's regular meetings - the monthly meeting with the superintendent, the high school principal, the elementary, and the junior high school principals of each high school attendance area within the district -was the least favorite of all of his meetings. (His criticism of this meeting was that the superintendent usually delivered a monologue about the school district rather than nurture an exchange of ideas) (95).

Activities

Elementary and secondary principals differ in the manner by which they conduct their tasks. Elementary principals tend to confine themselves to their schools. They are also likely to wish to restrict their responsibilities to their schools. For example, an elementary principal states, "The most important thing in my work is my school. I must see to it that the teachers are happy, the building functioning adequately, and that resources and materials are available. In fact, I would say that a certain feeling of possessiveness about the school is necessary in order to be a successful elementary principal" (January 1976).

Covell (1977) reports a similar remark:

Principals stated privately and two stated in principals' meetings that they "wish central office administrators would leave them alone," and not "continue to pile on work loads and interfere with the daily job of running a school." Another asked in a meeting, "Why don't you (central office) take on the business of collective bargaining and leave us principals alone to run our schools?" (126)

Wolcott (1973) reports likewise in the following passage:

Ed felt a perpetual sense of responsibility toward the school building. It was not unusual for him to go to the school or to drive by it sometime during the weekend, and occasionally he spent some time on Saturday in his office "catching up on the paper work" - that is preparing written reports (95).

Elementary principals, then, view their task as being more centrally focused on their school while secondary principals are oriented more towards the district. Elementary principals are engaged more often in tasks that are directly connected to their schools whereas secondary principals hold committee memberships throughout the district.

Opportunity

What about the degree of opportunity within the different principals' position? As was stated earlier, the elementary principalship is the least likely to lead to any other administrative position. It is also the position most likely to be permanent for its members. There are several reasons for this.

Where else can elementary principals move? They can go to the central office. However, movement into the central office does not necessarily mean assuming an adminsitrative position. Holding the elementary principalship does. This, then, leads to a tendency to retain the elementary principal's position.

The administrative position most likely to be held by women is the elementary principalship. Since most women do not assume an administrative position prior to about fifteen years of experience, those women who finally do obtain the position may not be especially desirous of continuing the upward move. Also, these individuals are now competing with much younger white males for the other positions. This contributes to the elementary principal's position being of limited opportunity.

The secondary principalship position, on the other hand, tends to be more fluid. The AASA study (1960) found that superintendents were more likely to come from the secondary school ranks.

Functions

There is another critical point that describes the differences between the principalship positions. The functions of elementary and secondary principals differ in certain aspects. First, elementary school days are normally confined to the regular 8:00 or 9:00 a.m. to 3:00 or 4:00 p.m. daylight hours. Special occasions such as holiday celebrations, yearly community functions, or special display activities are not common. Extra-curricular activities are usually confined to school functions and day-long field trips.

Elementary schools, in other words, do not participate in complex, long drawn-out, evening and/or community activities.

The secondary schools, on the other hand, have elaborate sports, music, drama, art and other special academic programs which extend the school day into the evening hours and the school week into the weekend. These functions afford the principal lots of visibility and risk. These elements of the position require support from the school district's leadership. This relationship thus insures that secondary principals are not only positively placed vertically and functionally but are also in a position to move centrally. The elementary principalship offers little opportunity for movement towards the center of the organization.

Centrality

The high school principalship, then, is the principals' highest hierarchical position. Its functions are not only related to the building site, but expand across the school district. But most important, it is the only position which moves the individual towards the core of the organization. It is the position which most likely provides for easy access to the superintendent and others in the central office; it provides the most direct linkage to the superintendent.

CENTRAL OFFICE

Other administrative positions are located in the central office. The central office is the hub of the school district's governance. School board meeting and work rooms and the superintendent's office are located there. All of the district's personnel and finance offices are to be found there, as are the instructional and support services. In addition, such services as research and evaluation, affirmative action, social welfare, and others may also be housed in the central office.

Administration Versus Others

Most positions in the central office are assumed after some teaching experience. Those positions which are designated as administrative require administrative experience and a State Administrative Credential. Since this study is concerned with administrative careers, the central office positions most intensively studied are those which are held by administrators.

The best indicator to distinguish those positions which provide the opportunity for attaining the superintendency and those which do not is the requirement of the administrative credential. Another way is to distinguish line and staff positions. Those positions which do not require an administrative credential are clearly staff positions. Those which do require an administrative credential may or may not be line positions.

The data for this study revealed four groups of central office personnel. McGivney and Haught (1972) and Gittell (1967) report on two major groups. Gittell also reports on the operational field staff. These two studies differ from each other in the size of the school districts studied. Gittell's study of the New York schools is a large city school district while the McGivney and Haught study is that a of a medium sized city (100,000 - 500,000 population). The differences between the central offices, however, do not appear to be significant. Moreover, McGivney and Haught conclude "that the COS influence on policy-making in medium-sized cities was pervasive (perhaps as great as that described by Gittell and Rogers (1968) in large cities)" (34). The present study's data, which include large and medium-sized school districts, also do not reveal significant differences between central offices.

There are four major groups whose primary distinction is that one is likely to provide the opportunity to obtain the superintendency while the other three do not.

Those careerists in the central office occupying the positions directly below the superintendency are likely to become future superintendents. They comprise the most powerful group in school administration. This group has three characteristics: 1) the interaction between it and the superintendent is continuous on a formal and informal basis; 2) its members hold less tenure in the district than do members of the other three groups; and 3) its reference group is the school board. McGivney and Haught (1972) describe this group in the following passage:

> This major subgroup has three characteristics: (It) interacts on a daily basis and in the weekly administrative staff meetings led by the superintendent; position holders have considerably less tenure in the district than do members of the second major subgroup, and its significant other is the board of education (25).

The second group consists of those careerists who are confined to the central office positions, i.e., they are not likely to become superintendents. Its two important characteristics are: 1) its members hold long tenure in the school district, and 2) its reference group are principals and teachers. The group retains its structure through informal interaction and regularly scheduled monthly meetings. McGivney and Haught (1972) describe this group in the following way:

> (It) interacted on a daily basis both functionally and socially, and officially interacted at a monthly supervisory council meeting; position holders hold considerably more tenure in the district than did members of the first major subgroup and, as one result of this tenure, showed a preference for the leadership style of the former superintendent under whom they also served; and its significant others were building principals and teachers

rather than the board of education (26).

The third group[1] is made up of those who hold the position of area administrator.   Area administrators are usually minorities appointed to contain the community.   These appointments are not viewed as rewards or as positions acquired due to outstanding accomplishments.   Because of the nature of the appointment, its significant others are community persons.   Gittell (1967) presents a description of school administrators who are similar to the area administrators presented above.   She refers to this group as the operational field staff.

The fourth group is made up of those who hold a variety of positions such as principal on special assignment at the central office.   The members of this group, like those presented above, do not acquire their positions as rewards or as a consequence of their superior performance.   Rather, they are individuals who have erred and for some reason, cannot be released from the school district. Their reference group consists of specified persons within their assignment.

In furthering the analysis of central office positions and using the major distinctions established above as starting points, we will now apply the theoretical framework to determine the positions' organizational characteristics.

Hierarchy

Hierarchically, those positions directly below the superintendency are few in number; tend to carry associate, deputy, or assistant superintendency titles; and command higher salaries.   In contrast, the second group tends to have more general titles such as director, coordinator, administrator, consultant, assistant director, or manager.   The third group is usually referred to as area superintendent or administrator.   This group is hierarchically placed below the two groups described above and below the principals.   Because its reference group is made up of community persons, its hierarchical placement is somewhat ambiguous.   The fourth group is usually referred to as "those on special assignment." Its organizational placement is ambiguous due to its assignment and to its reference group.   These individuals function more like staff members and may be considered as outside of the line hierarchy.

Organizational Space

Working Environment

The working environment differs in several important aspects. Associate, deputy, and assistant superintendents tend to have their own offices and secretaries located next to the superintendent. Members of the other groups tend to have combined offices with shared secretarial help and telephone service.   In addition, the area administrators and those placed because of their errors are usually located away from the two major groups and closer to other support staff housed in the central office.

Interpersonal Relationships

The opportunity for the development of intensive and extensive interpersonal relationships is obvious. Those individuals in the first group are located next to the superintendent and board of education members and furthest from everyone else. The data collected for this study indicate that with the exception of one (and this changed during the term of the study), the superintendents' offices were located on the highest floor of the district building while everyone else was below that. Holding these prized positions is proof of their extensive network of support throughout the school district. Reference groups or "significant others" are an indication of the quality of interpersonal relationships. The four groups differ in their "significant others". The first group's "significant others" are the superintendent and the school board. Principals and teachers are the second group's "significant others." The area administrators' "significant others" are community members. Gittell (1967) reports that this group's concern is "their public relations role" (82). These administrators agree that the principals are their particular concern. Few indicate that the supervision of teachers is a primary responsibility. The presently reported upon data are consistent with Gittell's findings regarding area administrators' contact with principals, which revealed a surprising lack of contact, except in formal monthly meetings. Individual conferences with principals are rare, evaluation scanty, and services to principals limited.

The fourth group's "significant others" are selected school personnel. Because their appointment is not viewed positively, these individuals are effectively kept from interaction with members of the two major groups of the central office and some building site principals. The critical characteristic of this appointment is that selected personnel are the only ones who interact consistently with this group's members.

Activities

The members of the group directly below the superintendent are the most influential in the establishment of school policy. They are equally influential in implementing the policy and protecting the school district. McGivney and Haught (1972) state, "In fact, it appears that those who are appointed at the pleasure of the superintendent and the board have reversed the assumed relationships and have co-opted much of the policy-making apparatus of the school district" (35). The nature of their task is clearly central to the organization.

In contrast, the second group conducts its major tasks with those outside the central office, principals and teachers. The major concerns are instruction, building site materials, equipment, and services.

The third group confines itself to activities related to containing the community. The members may indicate that they are most concerned with principals, but the concern is actually limited to seeing that community members do not bother principals. They represent the school district in community affairs, but cannot speak or act for the school district. Gittell (1967:83) also reports on the activities of this group in the following passage:

> When asked about activities on a typical day, these superintendents commonly noted visits to school and group meetings with staff. Such visits, however, have little to do with review of teachers, principals, or curriculum. Finally, meetings with parents and outsiders are more common than meetings with principals or teachers.

The members of the fourth group work on routine matters which confine them to a few selected persons within the school district.

Opportunity

These positions are, then, different in their content of opportunity. The first major group described above provides opportunity for the acquisition of the superintendency. But equally important, the position offers an opportunity for interaction among those who matter in the organization. It also provides an opportunity to engage in the most important functions of the organization.

The second group provides opportunity for stabilizing an administrative career at this juncture. It engages in worthwhile activities and offers support to the superintendent and his associates. On a very rare occasion, a member of this group may assume an assistant, associate, or deputy superintendency position. However, this possibility is unlikely since the positions occupied are more apt to be staff rather than line, and movement from one to the other is rare (Briner and Iannaccone, 1966; AASA, 1955; Pittenger, 1951; Etzioni, 1959).

The third group, on the other hand, is not expected to provide opportunities for permanence or for further movement in the organization. In fact, individuals occupying these posts don't appear to have acquired them as rewards. As stated previously, data collected for this study reveal that these positions are acquired by those whom it is perceived can contain community conflict.

Those individuals in the fourth group who have erred in the school system at some time, but for some reason it was not possible to remove them, are likewise halted in any further movement.

Power

Those positions comprising the first group are the "power" positions of the organization. Occupying these positions provides the individual with power absent everywhere else throughout the organization. The other three groups are subservient to the school board, superintendent, and his associates.

As has been noted, power has not been presented as an analytical descriptor of the previously presented positions. This is because power is absent in most of the educational administration positions. Its presence is, however, obvious in those positions occupied by the first group in the central office. There are several indicators of this power.

The first group is the group with the "ability to get things done" (Kanter, 1977:166). Since it has direct contact with the school board and superintendent, this is the body which creates, interprets and implements policy. For example, during a collective bargaining period in one of the school districts, the members of this group were in direct contact, reported to the superintendent and school board, and were responsible for the research and formulation of policy statements. These individuals were apprised of the progress of the negotiations at all points. No other group participated in the same manner. Even though teacher representatives were part of the negotiation, district information was never as readily accessible to them, nor were school board members as available to teachers as they were to the superintendent and his "first group".

McGivney and Haught (1972) likewise report:

> Since the COS controls a disproportionate share of the factors which influence policy outcomes (expertise, information generation, and control), its significant others, the school board and the superintendent usually defer to the COS proposals (30).

They state further:

> Over the entire period of observation no action was initiated by the COS staff at the official board study sessions. Moreover, no action was initiated by school staff at official board meetings. All actions initiated by outside groups either at official board meetings or at board study sessions were referred back to the board study sessions and, in the process, to the administrative council and the major and minor subgroups of the COS.

> ...(T)he COS seeks to present a united front to the board of education and to the "public" by controlling not only its own proposals, but by intercepting and controlling the proposals from other groups and subsystems within the school system, such as students, teachers and principals. ...Control over externally generated proposals is effectively met by the COS either by intercepting them before they are presented at the board study session or by taking

custody of them and submitting them to the (subgroups) of the COS for review, revision or rejection (32).

The first group is also able "to mobilize resources" (Kanter, 1977:166). Being just below the superintendent enables members of this group to command others in the school district to act and/or to redistribute goods and materials throughout the school district. For example, after much study and district deliberation, it was decided to adopt a new computer program for a high school in the district. The final decision regarding the school, the teachers to be involved, and the way the program was to be described to the school district's community was made by those individuals in the first group with the approval of the superintendent and the school board.

Another indicator of power in these positions is noting what its members do. First the individuals have not held their positions long. They take risks in making decisions for the school district. Also, they are aware of making decisions which have high visibility and which appear most appropriate at the time. The personal accretion of power in this manner usually means that these individuals will become superintendents. In the present study, every assistant, associate and deputy superintendent who moved into another titled superintendency or superintendency were high risk takers. (See Tables 8 - 12).

As a group, it was widely known and acknowledged that the informal political influence, outside status, sponsorship, and mobility prospects resided here.

In the quest for the superintendency, it is necessary to acquire power through others. Although individuals in the lower hierarchical levels may obtain power from others, their ability to utilize it is greatly constrained. The legitimacy is questioned and the context is likely to be improper. Occupying those posts directly below the superintendent does not pose this problem. First, the superintendent is available to grant power to these individuals. Second, being so close to the superintendent and to the top of the hierarchy makes it proper to grant power or it makes it proper to seize power. Moreover, continuous access to the superintendent and the school board makes it possible for power to be acquired through others in a legitimate fashion. All of these characteristics are absent in all other positions in educational administration.

In brief, the central office positions may be contrasted along several dimensions. Each dimension accentuates the distance from the superintendency and from the core of the organization. It also demonstrates that failure to move vertically, functionally, and centrally jeopardizes the acquisition of the superintendency and determines the quality of participation within the organization.

Central office positions differ in their requisite of an administrative credential. They also differ in their "significant others." One group interacts with the superintendent and board members within the same building and area. The other group interacts with principals and teachers. The third group interacts with those in the community. The fourth group interacts with selected ones within the school district. The combined characteristics contribute to important differences between the positions and differing consequences for those individuals occupying them. Table 2 illustrates the hierarchical rankings of the various school administration positions.

CONCLUSIONS

School administration positions have been analyzed in terms of their organizational structure characteristics. The underlying assumption has been that organizational positions contain characteristics which determine the quality of participation of individuals occupying them and opportunities for upward movement.

It has been seen how the vice-principalship offers an initial opportunity to depart from teaching and assume an administrative position. It has also been shown how the principalship positions differ in important aspects. Hierarchically, the elementary principalship is below the secondary principalship. The principalships also differ in their working environments with secondary principals heading more complex organizations. The opportunities for developing intensive and extensive interpersonal relationships for each principalship also differ. Secondary principals are favored in the amount and degree to which they can develop intensive and extensive interpersonal relationships. Likewise, the activities in which secondary principals engage differ from those of elementary principals. Elementary principals are more likely to remain confined to their schools whereas secondary principals are likely to participate on a district-wide basis.

Secondary principals are also more likely to move to the superintendency than are elementary principals. The elementary position is therefore more likely to be permanent.

Principals also differ in the functions they perform. Secondary principals' functions extend the school day and school week whereas elementary principals' functions are limited to day long activities. All of these characteristics contribute to making the secondary principalship position one that has not only moved the person vertically and functionally, but also centrally. The secondary principal is more likely to have a direct linkage to the superintendency.

The central office positions consist of four groups. The first group is directly below the superintendency. This group deals with the superintendent and the board of education. The members of this group are more likely to become superintendents. The second group is composed of staff members rather than line. This group supports the first group and it deals with teachers, principals and instructors. The third group is referred to as area administrators. The members are usually minorities who have been appointed to contain the community. Their "significant others" are community persons. The fourth group are those who have erred in the school district, but for some reason or other cannot be dismissed. Their

TABLE 2.   Educational Administration Hierarchy

Line	Line or Staff	Staff	Unspecified
Superintendent			
Deputy Superintendent;			
Associate Superintendent			
Assistant Superintendent	Director		
	Assistant Director		
Principals			
High School Principal		Supervisor	
		Coordinator	
		Consultant	
Elementary Principal		Manager	
		Administrator	Area Administrator
		Specialist	Administrator on Special Assignment

"significant others" are selected persons from the school district.

Socialization processes occur within the context of each of these positions in relation to the personal attributes of those individuals occupying them. This is the topic of the next chapter which attempts to show how individuals change administrators.

NOTES

[1]Gittell (1967) refers to this group as operational field staff and district superintendents. Subsequent to her study and reorganization of the New York City Schools, the decentralized structure retained the "district superintendents who were no longer chosen by test scores which have no relation to leading or administering a district; under the new law, local school boards hired their own district superintendents on a contractual, rather than a tenured basis" (Ravitch, 1974:398).

CHAPTER 3

Socialization Processes

So far, the school organization's factors which have a bearing on establishing educational administration careers have been described. The prominent positions have also been presented. But this does not suffice to explain how individuals establish school administration careers. Individuals have two options as they enter an organization. They may decide to establish a career in a given position, such as a teacher or an elementary principal. Or, they may decide to try to attain the highest hierarchical position within the organization. Either of these options presents a differing socialization process for the individual. The important difference between the two options is that those who choose to move to the highest hierarchical position must undergo severe changes as they climb. Those who opt to remain at any one level will change only to the degree that is required to keep the present position.

As was stated earlier, virtually all school administrators must begin by teaching. Therefore, entrance into the school organization is legitimately gained through teaching. As teachers, individuals are perceived differently. For instance, since it is assumed women wish to remain as teachers, the organizational lore encourages them to do so. Other characteristics of the position such as the retention of the school schedule remain attractive to women who can return early to their homes to prepare the evening meal. The consequence is that women are socialized to remain teachers. In contrast, white males are strongly encouraged to "move up" to administration. For example, a school personnel director said, "I tend to suspect white males who want to teach kindergarten. I can't imagine a man being happy doing that for a whole year. Individuals like that are different or weak" (February 1977). A high school principal describing a first grade white male said, "I can't understand how Carl thinks he can be a good first grade teacher. Men make better teachers with older students" (September 1978). An associate superintendent for personnel said, "Men are more likely to be good administrators. It is easier for men to manage and administer than to teach young children" (December 1976). From the statements presented above it can be seen how men are expected to "move up" to administration.

Organizational Boundaries

There are several elements which act upon the individual. These elements may be viewed conceptually as boundaries. Individuals either remain within the boundaries or cross them. Schein (1971) presents three boundaries which correspond to the three types of movement necessary in establishing a career. The hierarchical boundaries separate hierarchical levels. These are the boundaries which determine vertical movement. For example, moving from teaching to administration. The functional or departmental boundaries separate departments, divisions, or different functional groups from one another. The inclusion boundaries separate individuals or groups who differ in the degree of their centrality (404-405).

"Boundaries vary in number, degree of permeability and type of filtering properties which they possess" (Schein, 1971:405). Some organizations are very complex and the boundaries separating, for example, functions may be many in numbers. In school districts functional boundaries separate grade levels, subject areas, and specializations. In school administration functional boundaries are between teaching and administration and then between the various administrative units such as personnel, finance, and instruction.

Permeability

The degree of permeability is significant in that the issue is the ease or difficulty in crossing these boundaries. In school administration, for example, movement to the high school principalship is more difficult without high school experience. More immediate, school administration positions are more difficult to penetrate than others.

Filtering Properties

The particular types of filtering properties are also important to consider. Hierarchical boundaries filter in terms of attributes, such as seniority, merit, personal characteristics, types of attitudes held, and who is sponsoring them. Functional boundaries filter more in terms of the specific competencies of the individual or need for broader experience in some scheme of training and development. Inclusion boundaries are the most difficult to characterize in terms of filtering properties because the criteria may change as one gets closer to the inner core of the organization. Competence is critical in entering the organization, but such factors as personality, seniority, and willingness to play a certain kind of political game may be critical in becoming a member of the "inner circle." These properties may be formally stated requirements for admission or may be highly informal norms shared by the group to be joined (Schein, 1971:406).

Hierarchical Boundaries

In school administration individuals may cross the one hierarchical boundary from teaching to elementary principal and thereby develop a career. Or, an individual may opt to cross many hierarchical boundaries such as from teaching to high school principal, to central office associate superintendent, and finally to superintendent. In the ascent to the superintendent individuals must cross two hierarchical boundaries: from teacher to principal, from principal to superintendent or three which include teacher to principal, principal to central office, central office to superintendent.

Functional Boundaries

The functional boundaries school administrators may cross are more numerous depending on the complexity and size of the school district. The functional divisions include elementary and secondary principalships, many central office positions including the numerous associate or assistant superintendencies, and finally the superintendency.

Inclusion Boundaries

Various inclusion boundaries have to be considered in establishing school administration careers. The first is entry into administration. That may be crossed at the time the first administrative position is obtained. Unless school administration includes tenure in school administration, the granting of tenure cannot be classified as an inclusion boundary. Persons may have tenure in the school district as teachers, but may not as administrators. What this means is that in times of crisis, individuals may be demoted to the classroom rather than released, resulting in the termination of a career in school administration.

Crossing the inclusion boundaries in school administration is problematic. This study proposes that the inclusion boundaries exist in the principalship positions and certain central office positions. Acquisition of those positions moves an individual to the center or the core of the organization. The critical element is that the position must contrast in some way from the other positions at the same level to indicate inclusion. For example, an elementary principal gaining the leadership role among all other elementary principals has crossed the inclusion boundary. This leadership may be evidenced in terms of memberships in a critical district-wide committee or in representation of other elementary principals in various capacities. This would hold true for the rest of the principalship positions. In the central office those positions requiring an administrative credential, whose significant others are school board members and the superintendent, and those whose functions deal directly with policy, personnel and finance are inclusion boundary positions. The acquisition of these positions requires personal approval and support from central office personnel.

The inclusion boundaries are the most difficult to identify and measure because to a considerable extent their very existence usually remain implicit. The filterilng mechanism is difficult to locate because even the willing informant, including members of the inner circle, may be unclear about the actual mechanism by which people move toward the center. Even the concept of centrality is unclear because it does not discriminate between a person's feeling of being central or peripheral and some objective criterion of his actual position in the organization's social structure (Schein, 1971:408).

Schein defines "centrality" in terms of the person's position as measured by the degree to which company secrets are entrusted to him, by the ratings of others of his position, and by his actual power (408). The data reported in this study iindicate that the titles which indicate inclusion are principal and superintendent (all titles which include superintendent such as assistant superintendent, associate superintendent, and deputy superintendent). All other titles are not likely to be inclusion positions, but may become so under certain conditions. They are: director, specialist, program manager and head. (All of these titles were drawn from the California Public School Directories 1975 and 1979. The directories list all school site and school district administrative personnel in the State of California).

The most permanent titles of principal and superintendent can most assuredly be considered as "core" positions. When the title of principal is modified, however, such as vice-principal or continuation-school principal or adult-school principal, it is likely those positions are not "core" positions. The vice-principalship is not even a legitimate administrative post. Continuation-school and adult-school principalship positions rerquire irregular schedules. This characteristic would mitigate against their being "core" positions. The present study's data indicate that these positions tend to be granted to persons who have erred in the school district but cannot be dismissed for some reason or other.

School districts avoid a certain amount of ambiguity among central office positions by altering the titles as necessary. For example, the position of area superintendent. If those positions are meant to be "core" positions the title is retained. When these positions lose their "core" characteristic the title is changed as, for example, to area administrator. This is an indication that the position no longer carries "inclusion" responsibility. The net result is that the presence of superintendent in the title retains its original identity as an inclusion post. The data gathered for this study show that superintendents are aware of this characteristic. They were quick to point out that the "safest" position in the upward climb is that which carries superintendent. All other positions are suspect. One superintendent expressed it this way,

When you are bent on obtaining the superintendency the position most likely to head you off are those at the central office. As a secondary principal you and everyone else knows you're an administrator. That's not so at the central office. You may be given a job at the central office which looks plush but in fact is just a paper pushing one. Therefore, what you watch out for is to try to be appointed to a position which includes the title of superintendent. For example, it's better to accept the job of assistant superintendent than director. You know the title superintendent moves you closer to the superintendency. All other jobs, in my opinion, are suspect (April 1979).

However, there are occasions when other central office positions can assume "inclusion" characteristics. Consistent with Schein's (1971:408) definition of centrality, positions which grant a person extraordinary experiences, latitude of movement, multiple functions, secret information, and unusual influence can be classified as "core" positions. For example, a two levels below the superintendent director of elementary curriculum was not only responsible for the elementary schools' instruction, but was also assigned to the collective bargaining committee as assistant to the associate superintendent of personnel. In this capacity which combined both functions, he was not only granted routine experiences, but additional ones. Because his position spanned two functions he could also engage in activities which included the superintendents and school board members. He was exposed to district-wide information and could exert influence across the school district. Acquisition of "inclusion" positions involves the most extreme socialization processes.

Passage Through Boundaries

Socialization processes are actualized when individuals cross the above mentioned boundaries. Schein (1971:421) hypothesizes that the amount of effort at socialization will be at a maximum just prior to boundary passage, but will continue for some time after boundary passage. In regards to passage through functional boundaries, education and training play the major role. Organizational socialization occurs in connection with the passage through hierarchical and inclusion boundaries. This is true because the organization is concerned about the correct values and attitudes at the point where an individual is being granted more authority and/or centrality. Also, the person is most vulnerable to socialization processes at this time. He is anxious to move up or in, so is motivated to learn the organization's norms and values. He is also vulnerable after passage because of the new role demands and his need to reciprocate with correct attitudes and values.

Passage Through the Hierarchical Boundary

In school administration, passage through the hierarchical boundary is actualized as anticipatory and on-the-job socialization processes. Anticipatory socialization is the process undergone during the preparation for the acquisition of the first administrative post.

Anticipatory Socialization

Anticipatory socialization occurs at two different points in a person's career life. One is prior to teaching. These candidates assume teaching as a requisite stage but anxiously prepare to move into administration as soon as possible. The other point is after an individual has been teaching for a period of time and while there decides to become an administrator. Becoming aware of the aspiration towards administration at these two different periods produces two different comsequences. Those who enter teaching as aspiring administrators are able to maintain a detachment from the rest of the teachers so that when they do become administrators, their departure from teaching is non-stressful. Those who decide to become administrators after they've taught awhile experience stress when departing from teaching and other teachers.

This process is well documented in Blood's (1969) study where he reports on two types of candidates seeking the administrative role. The majority of candidates "considered teaching as a transitional role" (15). That is, of those individuals holding the principalship, most of them had aspired towards the position prior to teaching. Because the administrator position required teaching experience, these persons assumed teaching, but only as a necessary transitional step. They were never totally committed to teaching, nor did they develop loyalties and strong attachments for it.

The rest of the candidates were teachers, and as teachers they later moved into administration. For them, with developed commitments, loyalties and friendship ties within teaching, the departure into administration required greater degrees of alienation than was necessary for their counterparts. The changes necessary in these persons, i.e., the socialization processes which acted upon them were more severe than upon their counterparts.

Blood (1968) defines <u>anticipatory socialization</u> process as the "function of positive orientation to non-membership groups with consequences for the individual, his membership group, and the positive reference group" (16). That is to say, anticipatory socialization means departing from one group in order to gain membership in another. Stated another way, crossing the hierarchical boundary means leaving teaching in order to assume administration.

The elements involved in this process begin with the individual GASing, Getting the Attention of Superiors. Griffiths (1965) describes it:

A sizable number of teachers particularly men, seemed to do just about anything to get out of classroom teaching. There were the teachers who were GASing, that is Getting the Attention of Superiors. Those engaged in GASing are on appointment. They have regular teaching licenses and 5-19 years of experience. They took jobs that seemed to Miss A to be irritants: teacher-in charge of lunchroom, administrator of annual field day, chairman of teachers' interest committee, school coordinator of student teachers, or trainer of school track teams. There was not extra salary for these posts, but they all gave the incumbent a place in the sun, even though not a very prestigious place. While the jobs are not particularly significant, they do give the teacher an opportunity to GAS. Miss A observed, though, that these GASers were the ones who gained more important positions such as acting assistant principal, or, in the high school, the acting chairmanship. It is clear to the New York City teachers that to climb in the system one must first GAS (23).

As the individual engages in GASing, that is, tries to gain membership in a new group, steps must also be taken towards leaving the present group. Blood (1968:9) states:

> The norms of the culture and the profession are such that conformity to the norms of the teaching groups is demanded, and concurrently, the candidate must indicate a willingness to reject that set of norms for the norms of the administrative group in which he desires membership. (This) process appears to have the function for the individual of gaining entry to the positive reference group but with varying costs in alienation from the old membership group (30).

Part of this alienation process includes having the old membership group act to separate the candidate from it.

In the process of gaining membership to the new group, Blood found that access was a necessary factor. This access was facilitated by the presence of sponsors and those regarded as "others in the same boat," that is, other administrative candidates (10). The access was actualized through the cooperation of certain principals. For example, Blood (1968) cites some of his interviewees' remarks, "(The) principal recommended things - He encouraged me to get involved" (25). Another said, "She would let you in on things. She threw things my way" (25). Other ways of describing this process were: "(I) gained the principal's confidence. He could trust me. He extended his confidence to Me" (37). This special relationship between the aspiring candidate and sponsor reaped the benefit of access to educational administration. It also lessened the stress experienced by candidates as they left their former group.

Wolcott (1973:194) presents the sponsor's role in this process. He described how he had conspired with one teacher at his school to get the young man an administrative position. Their strategy was for each of them to take every opportunity to keep the sponsoree's name "in the fore" by having him named on committees and by giving him assignments that would constantly increase his visibility to central office personnnel and school board members.

Another way was to actually engage in certain activities. Blood (1968) found that those who had high access were "likely to engage in a greater number of administration-like activities resulting in (an) administrative perspective" (40). He also states that these persons "engaged in a set of non-teaching duties" (37). Finally, his report indicates that "access appears to be highly dependent upon the building principal. (It is) personalistic to the degree that it must be extended individually by the principal" (40).

All of the above elements contribute to fundamental changes within persons undergoing the process. For example, principals described teachers to Blood "as generally lacking understanding of the broader picture; of failing to grasp an aerial view of the educative process" (13). "Teachers holding the broader perspective would tend to be more understanding in terms of (the principal's) decision-making" (42). What is seen here is a change of attitude on the part of administrators where teachers are viewed negatively. conversely, these candidates, then, develop an "aware(ness) of the goodness of the administrative perspective" (Blood, 1968:43).

Another fundamental change was the acquistition of a new role in response to their job demands. They relinquished the teaching role to assume an administrative role (38). Blood explains that the teacher role "characterized by demands arising primarily out of interactions with an immediate set of students" is exchanged for the administrator role "characterized by demands originating from teachers, other administrators, and parents" (35).

The enactment of the new role (being a principal) carries the loss of coercive control over immediate subordinates and the lessened control over the work environment (63).

In summary, certain elements stand out as important in the socialization process undergone in acquiring the first administrative position. This may be conceptualized as anticipatory socialization. The process requires acquiring the necessary sponsorship. This sponsorship is actualized in the principal. Valverde (1973:36-37) states, "The key organizational position within the sponsorship model is the principalship." He goes on to state two primary reasons. "It places at the sponsor's disposal official power to grant training experiences to persons within the school, and two, it gives the principal access to central office personnel and information as well as other external contacts."

The sponsorship relationship consists of six different steps. The person is identified and the peer group (other administrators) grant their acceptance. The individual performs administrative activities.

Being successful the protege is adopted. Following adoption, serious training for compliance and assimilation follows. Fulfilling these successfully, the candidate is finally advanced (Valverde, 1973).

Anticipatory socialization has been presented here as that process which occurs prior to passage through the hierarchical boundary. However, conceptually, anticipatory socialization may occur prior to passage through any boundary. In this case, because the intent is to map out an educational administration career, this process has been allied to the hierarchical boundary.

As was mentioned previously, those individuals less attached to teaching experienced less alienation stress from teachers as they assume the administrative role. In contrast, those identifying most readily with their sponsor (the principal) assumed the necessary attitudes, personal skills and value systems with greater ease.

On-the-job Socialization

As candidates are GASing and engaging in administrative activities, they are acquiring experiences, knowledge and skills necessary for the upcoming position, but not until they ocupy the position can they actualize the role. Thus, during the early period of the assumption of the new role the candidate is heavily socialized. This process continues until the person is either secure in the position or it is decided he/she does not fit it.

Elementary principals tend to enter their positions from teaching. Doing so, their perspectives are directed toward the classroom, instruction and students. As they embark upon the principalship their perspectives change in accordance to the requirements of the position. The primary demands center around adult needs rather than those of children, school building maintenance rather than classroom, and a more ambiguous environment under the person's direction.

Mascaro (1973) found that when elementary principals first obtained their position their preoccupation was with four elements of their work. First, they "did not have enough time." This gradually changed to "not enough time to get into the classrooms." Second, "Getting into the classrooms" was viewed as an important activity of the principal's role. Third, they believed that change can be effected by the principal's personal involvement in the classrooms. And, fourth, they perceived that change should not be initiated until the principal has had an opportunity to become acquainted with "what's going on" in the classrooms and until the principal has been accepted in the role by alter role occupants (Mascaro, 1973:42).

As principals continued in their work their preoccupation with the original elements changed. The change allowed the principal to be satisfied with "a feeling" about what was going on in the classrooms (87). Consistent with this belief a de-emphasis of the importance of "getting into the classrooms" and a replacement of this activity with the practice of "going in and out of classrooms" took place. Subsequent to this a de-emphasis of the principal's personal involvement in the classrooms was accompanied by an indefinite postponement of effecting change in this way. This resulted in a de-emphasis of the need for firsthand knowledge of what is going on in the classroom, and a replacement of firsthand knowledge with information from secondary sources (87). As is evident, the resolution of the perceived original problems involved a change in perspectives.

The socialized principal developed a new perspective, one that recognizes that he/she is not only constrained by not enough time to get into the classrooms, but also by other factors such as teacher norms and central office directives which limit his activities as a change agent and leave him the options of either effecting change indirectly through teachers or teacher groups or to maintain the status quo, i.e., it permits the principal to be a change agent in name without the necessity of being a change agent in deed (123). In other words, the principal has become an administrator.

Several actors facilitate the process in becoming an administrator. Immediate and persistent ones are the teachers. Mascaro (1973) describes this influence on first year principals by quoting one principal's experience:

> The teachers' expectations were expressed in such ways as being told, "Manage; you run the show; we'll do the teaching. Run it so we don't have to complain about it so much, you know; but don't ask us for how we want it run, because we're not administrators; we don't want to make those kinds of decisions." And, yet in the same breath, the teachers' organizations say, "We want to have some say in it; we want to evaluate administrators (Mascaro, 1973:102).

The central office also socializes principals. It does so in a number of ways. One is by the evaluation process. Another is by monitoring deportment at general meetings. Still another one is by the manner in which it maintains contact with the principal, i.e., through memos, telephone, or personal interaction. Wolcott (1973) reports on similar means by which the central office socializes the elementary principals. He writes that general meetings were important places for instilling norms. The principals' evaluation conference with immediate supervisors was a powerful, stressful occasion. Seeking permission in advance and in writing forced elementary principals to remember who governed who. There were also formal and informal procedures which were used to control principals (221).

Other principals also act as the elementary principals' socializers. Whereas, the central office primarily socializes the principal through formal means; among principals socialization is predominantly effected by informal means.

Wolcott lists some of the ways in which principals were socialized by each other. Oral literature served to establish a tradition and topic of conversation. This enabled the younger men to turn to their more experienced colleagues when they wished to draw upon the accumulated wisdom of years of practical experience (221).

Another means was through the institutionalized use of humor. Wolcott (1973:223) states, "Like most school men, principals appreciated and encouraged the efforts of those among them who helped to keep school business from becoming unnecessarily serious and pedestrian."

As principals are socialized in their present positions, they also become aware of what lies ahead. Elementary principals soon come to know that there are "two routes up and out of the principalship...via a direct promotion into central office administration and obtaining a new administrative position or a post at a college or university. A third alternative was also possible. A principal could become active by seeking offices in his own professional organizations" (225).

As was stated earlier, none of these options is readily accessible to elementary principals. The result of this socialization is that they develop certain attitudes which guide their daily activities and contribute to making the elementary principalship a place to stay. Wolcott reports in his study:

> Virtually no advantage accrued to a principal of having his school in the limelight if the principal himself was already established in his career position. The way to "live and let live" was to run a competent and efficient school program, one that would keep a wide and disparate group...satisfied at best or, at worst, not so dissatisfied that they would organize and stir up trouble. I believe that Ed's effort and anxiety in his work as a principal were to a considerable extent aimed at preventing an event which never occurred during the study: a phone call from the superintendent asking or telling him what was wrong at Taft School (208).

High school principals are socialized by the central office, other principals and their teachers. In contrast to elementary principals, secondary principals are favored to a greater degree by central office staff members. This serves to maintain an hierarchically superior status and a more mobile attitude.

As a body, secondary principals socialize each other in much the same way as elementary principals. There is probably greater control among secondary principals however, primarily because the group tends to be smaller. Because of the greater degree of visibility and interaction with central office personnel and superintendents, secondary principals are less attached to their schools and are more likely to express desires to move elsewhere.

Teachers expect secondary principals to provide physical plant maintenance, material and equipment acquisition and protection from the community. Likewise, as a whole they do not depend on the principal for aid in instructional matters. They depend on each other, particularly on those of like disciplines (Charters, 1964).

In brief, secondary principals have autonomy and support from their superiors not granted as generously to their counterparts. They are apt to engage in risky ventures if they are reasonably secure in the central office's support, public visibility and the pervasive norm of movement. They are also more independent in their career mobility. The result is that secondary principals are not as likely to remain in one site, or to remain as principals as are their counterparts.

There is also another element to consider in the secondary principals' socialization. Since they administer schools which draw from a variety of communities, any segment of the citizenry is apt to change or place demands which could jeopardize their position. Therefore, secondary principals even if they are apt to desire to remain permanently in their positions may not because their general environment is not as stable or predictable as an elementary principal's.

Mid-Career Socialization

School administrators have several options in establishing their careers. They may desire to remain in their initial positions such as do the majority of elementary principals. They may desire to move to another position (normally a vertical move) and remain there for the rest of their career. Or, they may choose to attempt to acquire the superintendency.

Each of these choices carries with it certain consequences. As has been mentioned previously, elementary principals desiring to remain in their positions permanently adopt a posture which will not draw attention and which will serve to preserve their school and position. Secondary principals, on the other hand, remain wary and ready to move if necessary.

Those who are mobile within the system whether because they occupy precarious positions or because they eventually hope to attain the superintendency are socialized to remain flexible. This flexibility is maintained through several ways. One is to continually belong to district committees. If possible, holding an officer's position in these committees also serves to provide expanded and varied experiences. The participation requires knowledge of district-wide issues and insures that the participant will develop and maintain contact with individuals through the district. The socialization agents are therefore, others besides the central office superiors and building personnel. For secondary principals this activity greatly enhances their position and influence within the district.

Once the principalship role is mastered, socialization efforts on the part of the organization are diminished. Principals continue their work and barring severe organizational changes building site administrators are given personal autonomy.

Passage Through the Inclusion Boundaries

For those upwardly mobile administrators socialization processes continue. These individuals may move into the central office. The most common way to gain access is through the sponsorship of someone in authority in the school district. This may have been as a member of a committee or it may have been some well accepted school project. Gaining a position in the central office is generally viewed as an organizational promotion and places the person in view of the whole district.

The candidate confronts several changes. First, the working environment is radically different. The presence of students is rare, but the absence of adults is not. Finally, the constant presence of the school district's leaders is a potent reminder of the vast differences between the building site and the central office.

Second, the person's role has changed from that of an officer in charge to that of an officer among many. Most obvious is that the person is a newcomer. Therefore, a change in perspective is necessary, that is, the person is part of a team rather than alone. The individual must direct his/her attention to district-wide issues rather than building site ones. The welfare of the total district is the primary concern rather than that of a particular school. Also, instead of meeting teachers' demands, now the person meets the demands from competing groups: teachers, principals, board members, and other central office officials.

Central Office Staff (COS)

Upwardly mobile principals staff the central office. There are two types of individuals who occupy these central office posts: 1) those who obtained their present central office position as a reward but wish to go no further and, 2) those who are aspiring towards the superintendency.

Because most individuals don't acquire these positions prior to teaching and building site experience, these individuals tend to be older than those described earlier. Gittell (1967:9) in her study of the New York City Schools found that the central office consisted of the:

> system's supervisory staff developed completely through promotion from the ranks. ...Tenured supervisors hold top policymaking jobs. All assistant superintendents receive tenure after a three-year probationary period. The ingrown quality of the staff continues to increase.

She elaborates further:

> With the exception of two assistant superintendents who had experience in school systems outside of New York City, the entire core supervisory group was bred within the New York City school system - many as principals, almost all

with long experience at headquarters. A review of the background of the top supervisory staff members revealed that their careers followed a general pattern. Having served as principals or assistant principals, they were brought into the Board on special assignment and/or had served on special committees (usually as a result of contacts already established at headquarters) (11).

Two points may be made from the preceding passage. First, the central office is the power center of the district and second, entrance into these positions is by special assignment or reward. For these persons, moving into the central office - an environment of "old-timers" and district tradition can be conceived as crossing an impermeable boundary. The boundary is exaggerated for several reasons. First, as stated earlier, the central office houses the district's leaders whose power and influence has been increasing. Gittell (1967) goes so far as to state that the power of the central office has increased while that of the superintendents has remained relatively limited. She says, "In part, it is the very strength of the bureaucracy that has undermined the role of the superintendent" (8). This visible power is expected to impact upon newcomers with severity.

Second, due to the central office's composition of "old-timers" and "rewarded individuals" in the school district a prevading characteristic is its pertinacity. Gittell states that these members have developed:

loyalties which are strong and are based largely on who appointed whom. Top level deputy and assistant superintendents have moved up in the separate divisions of the system and their loyalties are based on their association in these divisions. Some individuals undoubtedly think they should hve been superintendent. This results in much back biting and petty jealousies (9-10).

Another characteristic within the central office is what McGivney and Haught (1972) described as their perspective:

We found that the central perspective of the COS was its need to perceive itself as in control of the situation. This unifying perspective resulted from the COS's attempt to reconcile two conflicting perspectives. One major perspective was the COS's self view as professionals. This perspective emphasized the COS's expertise in educational policy management and established norms for appropriate behavior of professionals within the school system. The second conflicting major perspective was that the school system operates in a "goldfish bowl" since it is perceived to be a public, open institution. These two competing major perspectives of the COS were reconciled by the COS to the extent that it perceived itself as having control of the situation (22-23).

The above described perspective points to significant changes which have occurred from being a building site administrator to being a central office position holder.

As a building site administrator, principals are reluctant to claim expertise in content areas. Their functions center around building maintenance and providing support and services to teachers. As central office administrators they must adopt a posture of expertise in various areas which is then claimed across the school district.

As building site administrators personal autonomy and anonymity were likely. As a central office position holder, the person is now on public display which serves to determine both the nature of tasks in which he engages and the manner by which he carries on his work.

Filtering Properties

Two reports (Gittell, 1967; and McGivney and Haught, 1972) describe the structure of the central office as composed of several groups. As was stated earlier in this report, the distinction between the groups is whether the positions lead to the superintendency.

Gittell's headquarters staff and McGivney and Haught's two major groups appear to be the same group. This group is composed of various superintendents and assistant superintendents who hold much of the decision-making power in the school district. They engage "in almost every area of school policy. They exercise power individually as heads of divisions and departments, and as a group they act to reinforce their individual decisions" (Gittell, 1967: 13).

For example, Gittell explains that in the selection of the superintendent the strongest institutional influence on the Board is the bureaucracy's (COS) pressure for an appointment of someone reared in the system. That pressure is direct and overt. It takes the form of direct recommendations in the public pronouncements of the various supervisory associations. Not unimportant, too, are the suggestions of individual members of the bureaucreacy that are solicited by Board members. The appointment of the superintendent so vitally affects the bureaucracy's vested interests that its concern is understandable (35).

McGivney and Haught (1972) describe their activities:

They control racial disturbances, the recruitment, election, and discipline of personnel; the allocation of financial material, and human resources; the preparation and transmittal (and withholding) of information to the superintendent, the board, city hall, the press, community, principals, teachers and non-professional staff; planning for the construction, repairs, restoration, and utilization of buildings, planning and programming the use of instructional hardware and software; and surveillance of potentially troublesome student and other groups (22).

The breadth of these activities illustrates several things: 1) the areas of expertise represented, 2) the scope of visibility, and 3) the variety of positions available to a candidate. Occupying those posts further removed from policy making, personnel and finances probably means a career within the central office without the acquisition of the superintendency.

Regardless of the position occupied, however, the candidate soon realizes that his/her behavior is under serious scrutiny. McGivney and Haught state:

> The perspective of professionalism permits the COS to view itself as having expertise in curricular, pedagogical, financial, and personnel areas. Given such expertise the COS creates rules and norms which place parameters around appropriate behavior for the professionals. Accordingly, it becomes unprofessional to criticize other professionals or board members in public. Professionals who violate this norm are severely sanctioned - even to the extent of socially isolating a COS member from participation in the COS activities (23).

Therefore, the central office serves as the place where the most rigorous personal requirements are enforced in order to belong.

How then, do individuals learn to behave within the acceptable parameters? First those granted admission are highly selected. McGivney and Haught describe how the COS regularly employed mechanisms or games in its hiring procedures. The COS exerts "control over the type of person who is employed in the school system - control beyond the amount assured by state certification requirements" (23). Or, the COS may "stack the deck" i.e., a person is placed in a vacant position in the COS itself (24). This is done through a judicious blend of formal organizational authority and through creative use of professional norms rather than adhering to the standard procedure in interviewing and selecting candidates for professional positions (24). Therefore, new members are individuals personally admitted by someone in the central office hierarchy. As was stated earlier, this selection process serves to reward individuals. Those individuals are perceived to resemble the existing membership and to be motivated to emulate those in control.

Second, individuals are placed in those positions where they can be closely supervised and with those whom they are expected to emulate.

Third, activities are assigned which will socialize them most properly for the role they are expected to fill. For those individuals likely to remain within the central office, activities with principals and teachers are maximized. For those most likely to acquire the superintendency, those activities which require continuing interaction with school board members and the superintendent are assigned.

Other considerations, such as variety in activities, expansion or restriction of their role, and multiple functions serve to shape the behavior of the newcomer.

From what has been presented previously, it can be seen that persons occupying central office posts find themselves in an environment which is more complex than that at the building site level. This complexity is actualized through the structure of the central office. Two major groups comprise it. The first group is that usually identified by the title of superintendent such as assistant, deputy or associate. It engages in personnel, budgetary, and policy issues. It interacts heavily wilth the superintendent and school board members. Future superintendents are drawn from this group.

The members of this group continue changing. Their position possesses the potential for achieving the superintendency. They will also experience the stresses associated with further rise. Their actions reflect loyalty and concern for the school district. They perceive themselves as leaders of a large, complex organization and they are prepared to face conflict and controversy. Those who fulfill these expectations successfully may become superintendents.

The second group is that which deals with all other matters of the school district. Its distinction is in the differing and changing titles and those with whom it interacts. This group interacts heavily with principals and teachers. These are central office careerists.

Members of the second group are socialized to remain in their staff positions and to aid the principals and teachers. Most importantly, they are the support system for those in the first group. For example, Briner and Iannaccone (1966) report in their study that "few supervisors had moved into the line-office hierarchy. Only two superintendents had been appointed from other than the principal's position in the past twenty years" (193). The justification for this structure is presented in the same work. They state:

> Specialization, to exist, must be embodied in the specialist as representing a particular aspect of the worker's general task; it must omit some aspect of the general task gaining in depth and uniqueness of skill and insight as it narrows in breadth and generality. To place the specialist in the chain of command over the general worker central to the duplication of labor in the work flow must result either in losing the benefits of specialization or reducing the scope of the worker's behavior to that of the specialist's only (197).

Indicators of Inclusions

Movement from the building site to the central office is an indication of moving towards the "core" of the organization. Several changes between the two posts are noted. First, the position is usually acquired as a reward or is associated with performing a special assignment, which leads to its acquisition being viewed as an improvement for the person. Second, the individual who acquires this position gains visibility and importance throughout the school district. Third, the person has moved closer to the superintendent.

Several factors aid in continued movement towards the "core" as the person becomes a regular central office member. In the study related to Walter, a white male newcomer to the central office, Ortiz (1979) reports that four socializing agents acted upon the subject. First, the leaders of the district acted as his support system. Second, the principals, the group he left behind, served to restrain his intrusion upon their schools. Third, the school board demanded thoroughness, display of district regulation knowledge, and district compliance. Fourth, an associate superintendent for personnel provided unique opportunities for participation in collective bargaining. The net effect of these socializing agents was that the candidate experienced competing and contradictory demands. The school board and principals served as restraining forces while the central office staff and the associate superintendent for personnel served as a liberating and supporting system.

The newcomer learned to function within the group along two spheres. As a school district leader he learned to work with principals selectively, preserving their school autonomy and providing solicited support. As a member of the central office he directed himself to emulating his superior and familiarizing himself with the total school district's functions. These two aspects of his work demanded that he understand building site issues as well as district-wide ones.

The successful candidate who crosses the inclusion boundary i.e., the person located at the central office who successfully moves to the center of the organization exhibits four characteristics. One, he is personally committed to advance within the school hierarchy. Two, he views his mistakes, experiences and shortcomings as a process of "learning." Third, he maintains a realistic view of the position, with its characteristics of limitations and possibilities. And fourth, he readjusts himself according to the demands of the various groups.

The organization aids in this process by: placing him in a position where he has access to those who decide "whom to move, how and at what speed" (Schein, 1971:401-402) one can advance. Second, the job is enlarged to include multiple functions. Third, the central office provides support and encourages initiative. And fourth, the organizational position provides both restraining and liberating forces which serve to train the individual to respond to competing demands.

As can be seen, crossing the inclusion boundaries of an organization result in fundamental changes on the part of the central office staff members. McGivney and Haught (1972) describe this in their statement regarding the potential for bringing about changed behavior among central office position holders through special training. They say:

The preponderance of evidence gleaned from the present study suggest that the on-going maintenance and refinement of group perspectives and processes is by far the more important factor, and hence the individual returning with new knowledge or training more likely will readjust to the on-going perspectives and processes (36).

Thus, the social system characteristics of the central office are powerful forces which impact on the behavior and attitudes of its members.

Failure to Cross the Inclusion Boundary

Not all central office positions serve the function of rewarding persons.   There are some positions which are granted for other reasons.   Individuals, former principals, or other school personnel may have erred and for one reason or another cannot be released. The organization finds a position within the central office bureaucracy for such persons.   This is functional because the organization is capable of controlling these persons' behavior while there.   There is another way to obtain a central office position which is not viewed as a reward.   If the organization detects a disturbance in the community someone may be assigned to contain it. The group comprised of these individuals appears to be what Gittell (1967) refers to as operational field staff.

In contrast to the two groups described previously, these other two groups are excluded from the "core" of the organization. There are several reasons for this.   First, as mentioned above, the members do not obtain their positions as rewards.

Second, these groups do not interact with school personnel. They tend to interact more heavily with community persons and engage in activities of greater import to the community than to the school district.   Or, they may be restricted to interact with selected groups within the central office.

Third, the positions do not provide opportunity for further mobility.   And, fourth, members of these groups face socialization in terms of failure rather than success.   Since the candidates located in these groups are viewed negatively by the school district they are essentially abandoned by it.   Socialization efforts are expended to insure containment of their negative impact on the organization. Those members who obtained their positions in order to control community disturbances may or may not be socialized towards advancement.   The members' efforts directed toward expanding their working relationships to school personnel may or may not be acceptable to the rest of the central office staff.   The critical point is that because the positions were obtained through another means rather than reward, all members of these groups are restricted to their present positions.

In summary, socialization processes in the central office take four major forms.   One form acts to prepare the person for the superintendency.   A second form acts to retain the person as a central office careerist. The third form is for those who have obtained their positions to contain community disturbances and the fourth form is for those who have erred in some way and it is decided the central office has the best place for them.

The Superintendency

Those who wish to become superintendents continue on their quest and they acquire the superintendency at an "average and median age of 51." Those superintendents reported upon in this study are similar to those reported in other studies. The most pronounced difference is that out of 20 superintendents, 3 are Hispanics. The other 17 are white males. In this sample, therefore, 15% are Hispanic. However, the Hispanic superintendents do not differ from the others except in age; they are slightly younger than the rest. They are in their mid-forties. The age most frequently reported in the AASA 1960 study was 54 (AASA, 1960:12). The same study reports positions in the larger districts were held by those who received their first superintendency at older ages. This may indicate a tendency for the larger districts to promote from within and to take more mature individuals for top posts (AASA, 1960:12).

AASA (1960) also reports that 38% of the superintendents have held the same position for the past 10 years or more (13). "On the whole, superintendents do not move from state to state" (13). The study being cited reports "85.1% had held superintendents in only one state, and a mere 2.9% had held positions in three or more states. Superintendents of large districts are much more likely to have moved across state borders than superintendents in small districts" (13). The median length of time in the present position was slightly under eight years (14).

Permeability

The experience normally undergone by superintendents is reported in the AASA (1960) study. They found 88.1% of the superintendents have been classroom teachers in the elementary school. 90% of the superintendents took their first administrative or supervisory position before the age of 35 (AASA, 1960:12). 82.5% have been building officials. The largest districts report 94.1% of their superintendents having been building officials. Two types of administrative positions have been held prior to the superintendency: a variety of building principalships and central office posts (33-34).

All superintendents in the present study have undergone similar experiences. The Hispanic sample as well as the others began as teachers, served as principals and central office holders before obtaining the superintendency.

Most superintendents, 17 out of 20 were high school principals. All of the Hispanic superintendents were high school principals. Half or nearly half of the superintendents in each population group reported upon by the AASA study were high school principals. Only one of the superintendents of districts of 500,000 population and over reported having been an elementary principal. Carlson (1972) says:

> In this generally uncomplicated trace from teacher to principal to superintendent, association with elementary schools seems partially to block movement of the superintendency; the elementary principalship seems especially to be a dead end for those aspiring to the superintendency (9).

In contrast, 16.0% of the superintendents in the smallest communities were one time elementary school principals (AASA, 1960:34). 22% of these superintendents reported they had at one time been elementary school teachers and 74.9% had at one time been secondary school teachers (36).

The sample of superintendents included in the present study were also representative of those reported in other studies regarding their previously held position. Out of the 20 superintendents, 2 had held a superintendency before. All had held an associate or deputy superintendency position prior to obtaining a superintendency position.

The positions held prior to the present superintendency as reported in the AASA study show that 46.1% of the sample had held a superintendency immediately prior to their present position. The smallest proportion moving directly from a former superintendency to their present post is in the districts of 500,000 or more population. Over two thirds of these men had moved from a position of assistant, deputy, or associate superintendent. This was also true of 36.9% of the superintendents in districts of 100,000–499,999 population and of 12.1% of all those reporting (36). 29.4% moved from the principalship (20.2% from a high school) to the present superintendency (36).

There is a definite trend for superintendents to move upward in terms of population of school district rather than downward. For example, 62.5% of the superintendents of districts of 500,000 and over in population came from districts of the same size (37).

The AASA report shows two patterns of moving through the ranks. 68.7% had held a central office position (assistant, deputy or associate superintendent) just before appointment to their present positions (38). No superintendent in a city of 500,000 or more population moved to the superintendency directly from a principalship, but 94.1% at some time had been principal, assistant principal, or other administrator in a school building (38). The most common pattern reported by superintendents in districts of 100,000 or more population was teacher, principal, central office administrator, superintendent. In the smaller communities the teacher, principal, superintendent pattern is more common (39).

The descriptions presented by the AASA (1960) and Carlson's (1972) reports show the importance experience plays in the various levels as a candidate ascends the superintendency. This experience can be viewed as the socialization process which the candidate undergoes through many years. The move is from the classroom/teacher/instruction to school building/administrator manager to district level/administrator/statesman. The changes increase responsibility, complexity, and breadth of coverage. The individual changes from being concerned with instruction and children to being concerned with an institution and adult groups. The individual's role changes to encompass school district policy and practice. These changes are continous and consistent. Most importantly, because the individual has been constantly crossing boundaries in order to keep moving, the stresses of organizational socialization have not subsided.

Filtering Properties

For those who wish to become superintendents, two courses of action are open to them. One is to wait until the superintendency is offered. The other is to seek a superintendency wherever it can be found (Carlson, 1972:39). For the first, the career is an ascent through the hierarchy in one school system, although he may have changed school systems earlier at some level beneath the superintendency (39-40). He is usually older than the man who does not wait when he takes office as superintendency from outside. His career is always spread over two or more school systems. Having been brought in from the outside, he has never served his new district in any capacity other than as superintendent. Ordinarily his career does not stop with one superintendency. To a greater extent than the man who has been promoted from within, he makes a career as superintendent rather than as a public-school employee (Carlson, 1972:40).

The two types of superintendents are called place-bound and career-bound. The place-bound superintendent is more interested in place than career and the opposite is true for the career-bound superintendent. The place-bound has a history in the school system and, then, has an established part in the organization's informal operations and activities. The superintendents in the present study were place-bound. Out of the 20 superintendents, 16 were promoted to their posts from within. They had held an associate or deputy superintendency and two were associate superintendents in other districts prior to their present position. The AASA (1960) report cites 35% of the superintendents were place-bound. 65% were career-bound. This is also supported by the Snow and Hickox (1967) report. They found 31% place-bound and 69% career-bound superintendents. Those promoted from within are over-represented in the larger systems. 17% place-bound and 95 career-bound work in systems of more than 100,000 inhabitants. 61% in cities over 500,000 and 46% in cities over 100,000 are place-bound men.

Since most of the sample in this study are place-bound men, their characteristics were similar to those described by Carlson. There was one striking difference, however. Out of the 16 place-bound superintendents, 14 held a doctorate degree.   The three Hispanic   superintendents   held   doctorates   from   prestigious universities.   Table 3 shows the superintendent's background.

Place-bound superintendents concentrate on old rules (93). Those rules they do formulate are typically related to the technical or   managerial   aspects   of   the   system   (96).   Even   so,   the superintendent's control is measured.   For example, Carlson (1972) says, "A chief executive cannot exert a direct, powerful influence in the management of internal group struggles.   He cannot act from within the group; he can only operate around the edges" (103).   One means he uses is to call on outside sources to apply some neutral influence.   Another   means   is   to   realign   the   membership   by promotion, demotion, reassignment, or dismissal, or removing the group leaders.   He can also apply two different strategies in order to gain compliance from both administrators and teachers.   Through the use of rules or rational legal authority he can gain obedience from administrators because they are more vulnerable to damage (Carlson, 1972:97; 104).   In contrast, he can apply "charismatic authority with the classroom teachers" (103).   Granting autonomy, encouraging participation in decision-making, and using committee procedures in problem solving or policy formation become his concerns (123-124).

Being place-bound means restrictions.   For example, Gittell (1967:10) wrote in her report of the New York City Schools:

> The procedures and influences in the choice of the superintendent precondition his ability to control the system he must direct,   His choice is so much dependent upon his ability to rise within that system that he can hardly be expected to challenge it once he takes office.   His own rise to power is an indication of his acceptance of established   interests   and   loyalties;   his   success   as superintendent is a further measure of his willingness to support and enhance those interests.

A distinction between superintendents is that "once a man has obtained   a   superintendency   the   career   ladder   does   not   end. Superintendents differ drastically, and there is considerable interest in moving to a different superintendency among superintendents (Carlson, 1972:10).   One reason superintendents continue to move is to achieve prestige.   The successful or prestigious superintendency is "determined by its standing on three general types of criteria: first, managerial responsibility as measured by the size of the organization, second, the quality of the school system in terms of "professional standards;" and third, the facilities available to the incumbent of the position" (10-11; in Mason and Gross, 1955: 328).

Therefore, it would be presumed that superintendents would tend to move from less prestigious to more prestigious posts.   This however, is not the case.

Much of the interoccupational mobility of superintendents is horizontal career mobility (from one superintendency to

TABLE 3. Superintendent's Background

	Average Age	Education	Elementary Teaching	Secondary Teaching	Elementary Principal
White Males	50's	13 Ed.D. 4 Ph.D.	3	14	3
Hispanics	Mid 40's	3 Ph.D.		3	

	High School Principal	Supt.	Associate Super.	Deputy Super.	Career--Bound	Place Bound
White Males	14	2	13	2	4	13
Hispanics	3		3			3

another of similar prestige) rather than <u>vertical</u> career mobility (from one superintendency to another of higher prestige). Men at the top of the prestige hierarchy of the occupation ordinarily start near the top, and men who start near the bottom ordinarily stay near the bottom (Carlson, 1972:13).

Carlson explains:

The position clearly seems to be one from which no man can emerge without some blemishes on his record; as standard conversation among school superintendents revolves around the uniqueness of their school system, suggesting that experience is neither cumulative nor readily transferable; and inasmuch as the necessary qualities and skills demanded by the position are at best very vaguely articulated, it is difficult to understand how experience might significantly contribute (13-14).

The present report indicates that the issue may be that the superintendency position boundary is highly impermeable. Carlson states that career-bound superintendents are significantly more involved in the network of interaction of the social structure and hold significantly higher status in the social structure of school superintendents (71). This appears potentially contradictory when this information is related to the acquisition of high prestige superintendencies. For those who desire to occupy the big superintendencies (100,000 -500,000 population) the most likely route is to wait for the position. The preparation for acquisition of the position takes place within the district. Transfer to another superintendency is likely to be of similar status. Therefore, acquisition of the higher prestige superintendency positions is most likely to be for the place-bound rather than for the career-bound.

One way to determine the direction of the socialization processes which superintendents have undergone is to examine how they resolve conflict. Gross, et al. (1958:251) in their study present four situations in which superintendents resolve role conflict in one of three ways: 1) to fulfill institutional demands; 2) to fulfill personal demands; or 3) to compromise between the two.

One of the recurring decisions with which they are confronted are those dealing with personnel. Gross and his colleagues found that the majority of the superintendents in their sample (85%) conformed to what can be described as the "professional expectation," 10% to the unprofessional and 5% compromised between the two (262).

Another type of decision which they must make deals with the way they allocate their time. Gross, et al. found that the majority of the superintendents (66%) conformed to the "occupational expectation" rather than to the "family expectation," 8% conformed to their family obligation, and 26% adopted some kind of compromise (267).

In the matter of raising salaries for teachers, the same study reports that 64% of the superintendents conformed to the expectation of recommending the highest possible salary increase. 9% recommended the lowest and 24.5% compromised (270). Finally, in the matter of giving greater priority to educational need rather than to the financial resources of the community 69% of the superintendents surveyed by Gross, et al. conformed to the "educational need expectation," 3% to the financial resources, and 27% compromised (274).

As can be seen by the manner in which the four conflicting situations presented by Gross, et al. were resolved experience in school administration group, the candidate has acquired a "professional" perspective. His actions are guided by that perspective. McGivney and Haught (1972) found this view highly pervasive at the central office. Therefore, school superintendents, due to the socialization processes undergone for a lengthy period, will, when confronted with personnel issues, be likely to take the "professional" stance.

Second, as part of this socialization process, persons who have continued to advance through the school hierarchy have systematically responded to the organizational demands of time. Their stay in educational administration has meant a continuing gradual increase of time allocation to their work. This is actualized as conforming to the "occupational" rather than to the "family" expectation.

Third, one of the requirements in the advancement through the school hierarchy is the development of loyalty and attachment to the organization's members. One indicant of this sentiment is supporting salary increases for teachers. The reciprocal response is subordinate support. This mutual aid is presumed to strengthen the organization.

Fourth, as members of the educational institution for several decades, superintendents' general priorities have been education. Their positions and their organization's well being are dependent on understanding what "educational needs" exist. It is therefore understandable that superintendents would tend to resolve a conflicting situation in a manner that would respond to the "educational need" expectation rather than to financial resources.

The point that is being made is that by the time a superintendent achieves his position, socialization processes have impacted upon his perspective, so that those demands most closely associated to his/her institution will receive priority. The fundamental change is that his personal decisions are in line with the institutional expectations.

SUMMARY

The socialization processes which individuals undergo as they advance within educational administration have been presented. Persons desirous of obtaining the superintendency position begin their career by teaching. During that period they engage in anticipatory socialization in order to depart from teaching and enter school administration. This is crossing an hierarchical boundary.

The first administrative post is likely to be a building site one. This may be as a principal. During the early part of the principalship, socialization is severe to insure the candidate's success. This is equivalent to crossing a functional boundary. Individual perspectives, tasks, and significant others change. The primary concerns change from classroom/instruction/children to school building/administration/adults.

Elementary principals are likely to remain at that post. Secondary principals, on the other hand, are likely to advance to the central office.

Obtaining a central office position requires personal invitation. Admission is usually granted as a reward for good work and the expectation that more will be forthcoming. This is conceptualized as crossing the inclusion boundary. Membership may be in one of two major groups. One group provides opportunity for the acquisition of the superintendency. This group's significant others are the school board and the superintendent. The major concerns are personnnel, finance and policy making.

Membership in the second major group provides opportunity to support the superintendent and the first major group. The significant others are principals and teachers. Their work is in all other school district matters including instructional and support services of all kinds. These are permeability and filtering properties characteristics.

Central office staff change their perspective from that of building site/administration/adult to school/district/professional expert, statesman/adult. Their concerns are varied and their efforts are directed to "control the situation" (McGivney and Haught, 1972).

A third group within the central office is for those persons who are placed there to contain community disturbances. It interacts with community persons. The fourth group consists of those individuals who have erred in the school district and there is no other place for him/her. Members of this group interact with selected school personnel. Their work is restricted. Opportunity for advancement is absent for the latter two groups.

The superintendency is finally acquired by a few persons who have ascended the hierarchical scale which has been presented. The position is obtained in one of two ways. The person could have received all of the necessary experience within a school district and waited for the positon to have been granted. Or, a person could have gone outside the school district to obtain a superintendency. The most prestigious superintendencies are those in large school districts, with professional quality working conditions and those with facilities available. Large school districts (100,000 - 500,000 population) tend to hire place-bound or those who have come up the ranks. After the initial acquisition of a superintendency, incumbents

SOCIALIZATION PROCESSES 53

tend to move horizontally rather than vertically. Therefore, it appears that those socialized in large school districts are more likely to remain as administrators of them. This means that persons obtaining superintendencies in small or medium-sized school districts are restricted to like ones for the duration of their careers. The permeability and filtering properties serve to perpetuate this system.

CHAPTER 4

Women in School Administration

As was stated in an earlier chapter, school administrators begin their careers by teaching. However, there is a difference between males and females in the way these careers develop. White males move into administration early, whereas a few women become administrators much later. The positions held by men are likewise different from those held by women.

Women enter the school organization in great numbers as teachers. For example, "data from the 26th Biennial Salary Survey shows that in 1972-73, the percentage of women in teaching was 66.4% (Meskin, 1978:323). Contrary to what would have been expected to be a positive feature for the encouragement of women to advance within the organization, there has instead developed a division of labor which has contained females in teaching and has fostered upward mobility for males.

Spradley and Mann (1975) state in their study of cocktail waitresses that, "the most frequent method of creating a division of labor employs male and female differences" (31).

> A latent function of this structure is that routine tasks become symbols of sexuality. The values that underlie feminity and masculinity are restated continously... merely by the act of working. (The result is that) as a symbol of one's sex, work is transformed into a ritual activity that announces to the audience of (parents, community and others) the significant differences our culture attaches to sexual gender(34-35).

In school organizations women instruct students; men administer adults. The many females focus their activities on students and instruction. The few males focus their activities around the management of schools and adults.

Education researchers describe the structure of the occupation. For example, Carlson (1972) writes:

> Because men are very much in the minority in public schools, because their ranks are rapidly depleted by those

dropping out of the occupation, and because they are advanced to administrative posts far more frequently than women, the men who simply persist in the occupation have a high probability of moving up the ladder. Thus, sheer perserverence seems to be a contingency of the superintendency; perserverence in an occupation that is highly feminized and in which men suffer "psychological and financial deprivation" (9).

The context, then, is created which encourages men to advance within the hierarchy while expecting women to remain in teaching.

A closer look at the structure of educational administration will reveal the stark division of labor between men and women. The greatest number of women in educational administration are at the central office. "NEA's data for 1970-71 show that 37.5 percent of central office administrators were female, 38.3 percent of the administrators in instructional and supervisory areas, and 48.2 percent of those in general administration." (Meskin, 1978:325). All of the above mentioned positions are staff offices. Occupation of line positions at the central office contrasts as follows: "2.9 percent are assistant superintendents, 7.5 percent are deputy superintendents, and 0.6 percent are general superintendents (25th Biennial Salary Survey, 10; Meskin, 1978:325).

NEA's statistics for 1972-73 show women holding 35 percent of the administrative posts in central offices, a decrease from the earlier figure; the data also indicate that the proportion of women assistant superintendents increased over the two-year period to 5.3 percent but that the percentage of women deputy superintendents and general superintendents again declined to 6.2 percent and 0.1 percent, respectively (26th Biennial Salary Survey, 9; Meskin, 1978:325).

Scriven and Nunnery (1974) present a more thorough breakdown of the positions held by women at the central office. Their study covered 26 school districts with pupil populations of 100,000 or more in the United States. The age range for their sample was from under 30 to over 60, with about 95% of the women being over 40 and about two-thirds being over 50. The median age for the sample was 53.46 years. Age was rather directly related to level of position. For example, the median age for those women holding assistant superintendent positions was 57.42 years, whereas the median age for those holding specialist consultant positions was 45.61 years. About 70 percent were currently married, 18.44 widowed, and 8.37 percent divorced (138).

All of the women had earned masters degrees and more than one-half of them held higher degrees. (The specialist was the highest degree held by 27.93 percent while the doctorate had been earned by 25.14 percent.) About 60 percent of the graduate degrees represented majors in some area of professional education, with educational administration and elementary education being predominant (139).

These findings indicate that the women who occupy these positions represent the broader spectrum of women. Women who are single, who may feel more strongly about career development are found in other administrative positions. An examination of the other administrative positions is in order.

The NEA 1970-71 report shows that even though "67.2 percent of the teaching positions in the United States were filled by women, only 15.3 percent of the principalships were held by them. Of these, women held 21 percent of the elementary, 3.5 percent of the junior high school, and 3 percent of the high school principal's positions. In addition, women comprised only 15 percent of the corps of assistant principals that year" (25th Biennial Salary Survey, 1971:10; Meskin, 1978:323). Data from the 26th Biennial Salary Survey shows that in 1972-73, the percentage of women in teaching had diminished slightly, to 66.4 percent, but that the percentage of women principals had shrunk to a greater extent - from 15.3 percent to 13.5 percent of the total group. Women according to the later statistics, now represented 19.6 percent of the total group of elementary principals. The percentage of women serving as assistant principals likewise decreased over the two-year period - from 15.0 percent to 12.5 percent of those holding the position (26th Biennial Salary Survey, 9).

This steady decline is also shown in "The Department of Elementary School Principals" of the NEA's Elementary School Principalship in 1968. It is reported that the woman "supervising principal" comprised 55 percent of the elementary principalship corps in 1928, 41 percent in 1948, 38 percent in 1958, and 22 percent in 1968.

The high school level shows a similar pattern. The Study of the Secondary School Principalship, published by the National Association of Secondary School principals (Hemphill, et al., 1965), indicates that in 1963, 11 percent of all high school principals were women. NEA salary surveys show the women represented only 3 percent in 1970-71 and 1.4 percent of all high school principals in 1972-73 (Meskin, 324). Over 50 percent of the women who fill these positions are single (Hemphill, et. al., 1962; Gross and Trask, 1976). Table 4 illustrates the contrasting findings.

What is revealed in this analysis is that many females occupy the teaching and the staff central office positions. Few females occupy the principalship and the line central office positions. Women, even though advanced into administration, continue to maintain instruction and students as part of their work. Men, on the other hand, depart from instruction and students and assume administrative and managerial duties among adults. Another difference is also revealed. Those women holding the staff positions are more likely to be married; those women holding the line positions are more likely to be single.

TABLE 4. Women in School Administration

	NEA 1963	NEA 1970-71	NCAWE* 1971	NEA 1972-73	Scriven & Nunnery 1974
Teachers		67.2%		66.4%	
Vice-principals		15.0%		12.5%	
Principals		15.3%	29.8%	13.5%	
Elementary Principals		21.0%	36.5%	19.6%	
Junior-high Principal		3.5%	13.9%		
High School Principal	11.0%	3.0%	9.1%	1.4%	
Central Office		37.5%		35.0%	
Special Support Services					18.44%
Community and Public Relations					2.23%
Special Consultants					11.73%
Coordinators					17.32%
Supervisors					30.73%
General Administration		48.2%			16.20%
Instruction and Supervision		46.3%			63.13%
Pupil Personnel		38.3%			
Directors					24.02%
Assistant Superintendents		2.9%		5.3%	16.02%
Deputy Superintendents		7.5%		6.2%	
Superintendents		.6%		.1%	

PASSAGE THROUGH THE HIERARCHICAL BOUNDARY

Permeability

When women enter teaching, the general expectation is that they will remain there. Three features exist which aid in the perpetuation of this system. Women continue to be prominent in schools particularly at the elementary levels. Second, it is perceived that women are appropriate for teaching children. Third, those women who express desires for administrative posts are restrained in one way or another.

One of the ways by which the expectations for women are actualized is through the granting of tenure after three years of successful teaching. In general, the granting of tenure to women is accomplished with relative ease. If, however, there is some indication from these women that they may move into administration, the granting of tenure becomes problematic. In this study, 30 out of 55 aspiring administrators related some difficulty in obtaining tenure. For example, a female principal stated:

When I first started teaching, I knew I wanted to be an administrator. Like a fool, I told everyone how anxious I was for tenure so I could apply for an administrative position. During my third year at the school, the principal called me in. He said, "I know you'd be happier in a different working situation than teaching, so I'd like to tell you that you are not expected to get tenure this spring (April, 1975).

Another female principal referring to her early aspiration said:

I learned early on that women aren't expected to aspire to administrative positions. I decided to keep quiet, get experience and an administrative credential and wait for a position somewhere (March, 1976).

Women, then, learn that if they wish to obtain tenure in a school district, they must suppress their aspirations regarding administration. They concentrate on teaching. If they wish to obtain an administrative credential and an advanced degree, they do so without alerting anyone of their long range plans. One associate superintendent said:

I realized that I had to leave the school district. I had told many persons I wanted to be a principal. The principal told me, "You can't fulfill your teaching obligations if you're preoccupied with becoming an administrator. I am therefore recommending that you not get tenure. It would be best for you, however, to resign and get another job somewhere else." I resigned, moved to another school district and believe me I just concentrated on getting tenure. No one ever suspected I wanted to be an administrator. I got tenure and then I felt somewhat freer to do other things (January, 1978).

TABLE 5. Tenure Acquisition by Aspiring Women

Total Women	Aspiring Women	Difficulty with Tenure	Tenure not Granted 1st District
127	55	30	20

Both men and women within the social system act to contain women within teaching. Greenleaf (1973-74) states, "For some reason many women resent the woman who seeks an administrative role and, rather than give her support, are more likely to accept her negatively. The remark is often heard, "Oh, she's playing the game."

Kanter (1977:218) cites an example about how men feel when women are bent on advancing. She writes:

And a number of men were concerned that women would jump ahead of them. They made their resentments known. One unwittingly revealed a central principle for the success of tokens in competition with dominants: to always stay one step behind, never exceed or excel. "It's okay for women to have these jobs," he said, "as long as they don't go zooming by me."

The point being made here is that women are likely to experience difficulty in acquiring tenure if it is believed they wish to advance. One male principal put it this way, "Teachers who start out thinking they're going to be administrators aren't as committed to children and their learning problems. Those persons just aren't as successful in the classroom." When asked if male teachers who wanted to be administrators were successful teachers or not, the principal retorted, "Men are aggressive. It's natural for them to want to advance and they're probably anxious about it too" (November, 1976).

One study (Colombutos, 1962:68) reporting on teachers found that only two percent of women teachers aspired to an administrative position, while almost half of the men wanted to become school administrators. Mason (1961:62) however, found that women do not enter teaching with this attitude. Beginning women teachers were more eager to achieve an administrative position than were the more experienced women teachers.

Another study showing similar results is that conducted by Greabell and Olsen (1973) who questioned 187 females and 20 males from a Florida Metropolitan school district regarding their desires to move into school administration. 32.2 percent of the 20-29 year old women, 22.2 percent of the 30-39, 9.3 percent of the 40-49 and 12.4 percent of the 50-63 women responded they would go into administration if they were given the opportunity. Contrasted to 65 percent of the males, the researchers concluded that women weren't as upwardly mobile as males. This researcher would say that a different interpretation of the data reflects the reality of the schools' perceptions regarding women in administration. The newcomers or the youngest group of women are less cautious in expressing their aspirations, so that approximately a third of them admit being desirous of administrative careers (135). The longer they remain as teachers, the more cautious they become about expressing their aspirations. Also, as they settle into teaching, many may see the upward climb as unrealistic for them.

Analytically, this can be seen as anticipatory socialization which requires gaining acceptance into a new group and departing from the present one. This process means that for women certain serious role stresses present themselves. First, the organization has been socialized to expect certain behaviors and attitudes from women. Desiring to administer and manage and departing from children and teaching are characteristics which are problematic for organizational superiors to accept. Second, departure from children and teaching is disturbing to women who have been socialized to be attached to them. Third, women who view themselves within the cultural definition of being feminine may experience role conflict in accepting women who do not behave within the cultural norms. Furthermore, the conflict would increase if a requirement of their occupation is to behave outside of the cultural norms. These aspects of assuming an administrative position are actualized in resistence from the teaching ranks to release women and the hesitancy from the administrative ranks to accept them.

In summary, women enter the educational organization as teachers. Their acceptance is assured as long as their aspirations don't include advancement into administration. The first indication of any resistance to aspiring female administrators is the denial of tenure in the school district.

Those women who are successful teachers and who do obtain tenure proceed to establish their careers at the classroom level. The potential movement is from less desirable schools and classrooms to more desirable ones within the district (Becker, 1952). After successful experience at the classroom level for ten to fifteen years, some of these women may become administrators.

As was stated earlier, the first administrative position for white males is usually the principalship. As was pointed out, women are more likely to be assigned an administrative position at the central office.

Filtering Properties

In a previous chapter it was reported that white males engage in anticipatory socialization, i.e., GASing in order to get the attention of superiors for possible access to the principalship. Women engage in this practice, but as just seen, it must be done after tenure has been granted. Even so, engaging in these activities is not favorably looked upon.

Kanter (1977) describes in her study of corporate life the manner by which women seek advancement. She presents an example in which middle managers contrasted two women: one who actively sought advancement and the other who did not. She states:

> One was liked by her peers even though she had an outstanding record because she did not flaunt her successes and modestly waited her turn to be promoted. She did not trade on her visibility. Her long previous experience in technical work served to certify her and elicit colleague respect, and her pleasant but plain appearance and quiet dress minimized disruptive sexual attributes. The other was seen very differently. The mention of her name as a "star performer" was accompanied by laughter and these comments: "She's infamous all over the country. Many dislike her who have never met her. Everyone's heard of her whether or not they know her, and they already have opinions. There seems to be no problem with direct peer acceptance from people who see her day-to-day, but the publicity she had received for her successes has created a negative climate around her." Some thought she was in need of a lesson for her cockiness and presumption. She was said to be aspiring too high, too soon, and refusing to play the promotion game by the same rules the men had to use: waiting for one's turn, the requisite years' experience and training. Some men at her level found her overrated and were concerned that their opinions be heard before she was automatically pushed ahead. A common prediction was that she would fail in her next assignment and be cut down to size. The managers, in general, agreed that there was backlash if women seemed to advance too fast (218).

The above passage illustrates how women are perceived within the organization and what it means for them in order to be successful. What it means for women in educational administration is that they must as teacher unobtrusively and technically excel in order to <u>safely</u> Get the Attention of Superiors. The more direct consequence is that their way out of the regular classroom will be by becoming some sort of a specialist. The general positions which are available are: reading, special education, or some other school related activity specialist. By obtaining an area of expertise, women gain legitimacy in order to justify actions from superiors in placing them outside of the classroom.

Two general patterns follow this practice. Women may be placed at the central office or at a school site. The requirement of an administrative credential for the position increases the likelihood that they will be placed at the central office.

An analysis of this position will help in understanding the socialization processes undergone.

PASSAGE THROUGH THE FUNCTIONAL BOUNDARIES

The Specialist

Women depart from their teaching careers by assuming a position which denotes specialization in some curricular area. Reading is a particularly popular area in elementary schools. The fine arts is a common area in secondary schools. Specialists may be housed at either the central office or a particular school. Elementary specialists tend to be housed in building sites. Secondary specialists tend to be housed at the central office.

Hierarchy

The position of the specialist is an ambiguous one. It may or may not require an administrative credential. The specialist reports to one of several superiors: the building principals, central office coordinators or to both. If the specialist is housed in a school building, it is likely the principal acts as her superior. If the specialist is housed at the central office, then a central office official is likely to act as her superior. It is not, however, uncommon for these specialists to be evaluated by several principals and central office position holders. This means that specialists are just above the teachers hierarchically but below the principal. In some cases, specialists may be considered as being on the same level as principals but as staff members rather than as line officers of the organization. In this case, central office personnel are responsible for evaluating them.

Organizational Space

Working Environment

The working environment of the specialist is diffused and differentiated. Several important differences exist between these positions and that of the teacher. First, specialists may or may not perform their tasks from a permanent classroom. When they do have permanent classrooms, students and teachers move in and out of them during the day. Another arrangement may be that the specialist goes to other teachers' classrooms and conducts her tasks from there. Still, another arrangement may be that the specialist uses several classrooms or instructional sites between several schools. In that case, both the specialist and teachers and students move in and out of classrooms during the day. A fourth way is where specialists are available for consultation to teachers. The consultation may take place in the supervisor's office or at the teachers' school or classroom. Principals may also call on specialists for particular help in certain areas. This means that the working environment for specialists is varied, indefinite and in many cases borrowed. (For a detailed study of specialists see Reed 1980).

Interpersonal Relationships

The most fundamental change which occurs when a teacher becomes a specialist is the addition of adults to the work load. Even though many specialists continue teaching students, in all cases they must interact with teachers. This is so because the students are not the specialists' but rather the teachers' responsibility. This means that at the very least the specialist must now establish a working relationship with teachers.

The relationship between the specialist and the principal also changes. A new structure emerges which allows the principal to assume administrative and managerial responsibilities and the specialists to engage in instructional supervision. These changes create a critical problem for specialists in determining who evaluates their work and effectiveness. They may have several persons who "report" on their effectiveness including principals and various central office staff members.

The crucial difference in this assignment is that the specialist role does not necessarily mean departing totally from the classroom, instruction, and children, but it does mean increased interaction with adults. The adults are usually teachers, but may also be other specialists and other central office personnel. In this way opportunities for developing extensive interpersonal relationships are increased. Also, the specialist has new and expanded occasions to develop intensive interpersonal relationships with the principals and central office staff.

Activities

Specialists engage in various kinds of activities. Some continue teaching students in large or small groups depending on their specialty. For example, a mathematics specialist might teach a concept to combined classrooms consisting of 90 students while a learning disabilities specialist might teach highly specific skills to one or two students. These activities lead to two quite different consequences. Whereas, the mathematics specialist has wide visibility and opportunities for interaction with many, the learning disabilities specialist may be highly restricted to her laboratory setting. Another consequence is that the activities are predominantly instructional and oriented towards children. This is antithetical to an administrative career.

There is also another type of activity in which specialists might engage. This is in coordinating the instruction of their particular specialty.   The primary activities include scheduling of classes and students, helping teachers and performing regular administrative duties.   They may be responsible for developing curricular plans, writing curriculum guides, preparing and ordering materials and equipment.

A third activity in which these specialists may engage in is administering particular local, state and/or federal programs.   This requires proposal writing, program monitoring, and program evaluation.   As specialists increase their involvement in programmatic activities, they decrease involvement with students and instruction.   This preoccupation with programs is more closely akin to administration.   For example, 1) interaction with "program oriented" specialists increases, 2) interaction with school officials responsible for program funding, implementation and evaluation increases, and 3) more time is spent in "an office" preparing reports.

In brief, the activities in which specialists engage are increased in complexity due to the addition of adults to their work. Activities may be of two major sorts: instruction or program administration.   Those who engage in instruction may deal with either large or small groups and with many or few teachers.   Those who engage in program administration are usually housed at the central office, operate from an office, and deal with other specialists and central office position holders.   The activities associated with program administration are more closely allied to an administrative role than those associated with instruction.

Opportunity

The specialist role does provide several opportunities for women.   First, there is at least partial departure from the classroom and instruction.   Second, the role has changed in regard to the relationship to other teachers.   Third, it is a post which provides increased visibility and schedule flexibility.   Those specialists who engage in instruction are not as likely to become administrators.   Those specialists placed at the central office and who are engaged in program-associated activities may become administrators.   The supervisory and other staff positions within the central office are also more readily accessible to the latter group. Specialists can advance to become supervisors and to hold higher ranking staff positions within the central office hierarchy. However, this advancement may or may not be readily apparent to district personnel which contribute to an ambiguous perception of the position.

SUPERVISORS

Supervisors are normally former specialists.   The supervisory post is usually acquired as a reward for work well done as a specialist.   Supervisors are likely to be those former specialists housed at the central office. Outstanding specialists such as in music or art, though, may receive unusually strong support from their communities and even if based at some school may obtain a supervisor's position. Supervisors seldom come directly from the classroom. They may have held an elementary principalship position.

Scriven and Nunnery (1974) in their report based on a survey conducted in the spring of 1973 was designed to identify and examine selected characteristics and perceptions of a sample of women holding central office administrative positions in the 26 largest school districts in the United States (those districts having a pupil population of 100,000 or more). From district provided data, a listing of women holding central office administrative positions was prepared for each of the 26 districts. From each listing, eight persons were selected at random to be surveyed. The primary means of gathering the data from the sample of 208 women was a 42-item (39 forced-choice and three open-ended items) instrument. The usable response rate to the mailed instrument was 89.06 percent (179 of the 208 women sampled) (138).

Scriven and Nunnery report that practically 96.08 percent of the women had been teachers prior to assuming administrative positions. 82.01 percent reporting having had more than six years of teaching experience and 10.62 percent reporting having had more than 20 years. (The median years of teaching experience was 11.89). Of the women, 41.86 percent reported that their teaching experience had been at the elementary school level. The remaining women reported teaching experience distributed among 15 subject areas, with mathematics and English being the most frequently mentioned. Almost two-thirds (64.80 percent) of the women had had no administrative experience prior to assuming their present jobs,[1] while another 26.82 percent had held one other administrative post. Of the women who had had prior administrative experience, over one-half had been elementary principals. The ages of the women at the time of appointment to their first administrative position ranged from 24-53, with 59.95 percent having received the first appointment between the ages of 28 and 39. (The median age at first appointment was 34.89 years.) More than one-half (51.96 percent) of the women had had all of their professional experience in a single school district, 19.55 percent had worked in two districts, and 12.28 percent reported experience in five or more districts (139).

The position titles that these women held were "assistant superintendents - 16.20 percent; directors - 24.02 percent; supervisors - 30.73 percent; coordinators - 17.32 percent; and specialists-consultants - 11.73 percent" (139). The areas of service in which women were found were: "general administrative services (personnel, finance) - 16.20 percent; curriculum and instruction - 63.13 percent; special support services (media, foot service, psychological services) 18.44 percent; and community and public relations services - 2.23 percent" (139).

Hierarchy

The supervisory role is encompassed in many titles such as coordinator, director and assistant administrators. Generally, supervisors and principals are at about the same hierarchical level. the chief distinction between them is that supervisors are staff officers whereas principals are line officers.

In the present study, all supervisors, even though holding an administrative credential, felt that they functioned as staff administrators rather than as line officers. Likewise, in describing the central office staff, Scriven and Nunnery (1974) state that about two-thirds (65.36 percent) of the women viewed themselves as functioning as staff administrators, and the remaining women saw themselves in line roles. Also, all women in the present report's sample reported to white males. For more than one-half of the sample (53.07 percent), Scriven and Nunnery report that the immediate superior was either the superintendent or a first-level subordinate (for example, associate, assistant superintendent). Almost all (92.74 percent) of the women reported that their immediate supervisor was male (139).

In the present study, all of the women worked with principals. Scriven and Nunnery report similar findings. Their respondents worked most directly with principals (25.45 percent), other central office staff (24.79 percent) and teachers (23.46 percent). They supervised directly from two to 26 persons (76 percent of whom were female), with the average being five persons (139).

Briner and Iannaccone (1966:192) report on the differences between secondary supervisors and principals. They state, "In the chain of command, the principal and supervisor appeared as classical line and staff officers." They summarized the hierarchical placement of supervisors and principals in the following passage:

> That is, each office in working with a common subordinate (teacher) and a common superordinate (associate superintendent) was capable of exercising two bases of social power or source of influence - 1) status as legal authority legitimated by general acceptance of impersonal rules, and 2) personal prestige derived from the quality of technical knowledge (193).

Organizational Space

Because the central office encompasses varying types of functions, a variety of positions are available. The functions range from student services to building maintenance and community relations.

Working Environment

Supervisors are generally housed at the central office. They are usually grouped in some manner so that secretaries, telephones and other services are shared. Briner and Iannaccone (1966) in contrasting principals and supervisors write:

> Principals' officers were larger and better equipped for study and conferences. Clerical and staff assistance was more readily available to principals for planning and conducting professional meetings, opinion surveys, and research efforts. These status symbols were visible expressions of promotional achievement in the administrative hierarchy (193).

Interpersonal Relationships

Because supervisors deal primarily with instructional matters, their "significant others" are principals and teachers. However, being placed at the central office does not provide opportunities to interact with central office superiors. In detailing the interpersonal relationships necessary in their work, Briner and Iannaccone (1966) present a description on time allocations to the various groups which interact with principals and supervisors.

> Within schools, the principals spent the most time with assistant principals, secretaries, and head counselors regarding school business and much less time with department chairmen. The supervisors interacted most with teachers and department chairmen and less with assistant principals. Outside the school, the principals spent the most time with the assistant superintendent for secondary education, the administrator of assignments, and those involved with managerial functions. Supervisors interacted most with other subject supervisors, high school principals, the administrator of assignments, and the assistant superintendent. The work-association patterns of principals and supervisors within schools seemed negatively related. The supervisors spent more time with teachers than with assistants to the principal, whereas the converse was true of principals. Also, the supervisors spent more time conducting their business with principals than did principals with supervisors. Similar accounts of time were spent by both with the assistant superintendent and administrator of assignments (194).

> In amount of time spent, supervisors worked primarily with principals as well as teachers, whereas principals worked secondarily with supervisors and teachers. These relationships existed in spite of the same organizational level of both offices, as indicated by almost equivalent times spent by each with the associate and assistant superintendents (195).

The above indicates that supervisors' interpersonal relationships are confined to those most directly involved with instruction and students.

Activities

Most supervisors deal with instructional matters.   This might include resource allocation and district-wide scheduling of the various instructional activities.   (Those supervisors dealing with transportation, cafeteria management, etc., engage in activities quite distinct from those this report is most concerned about.   Only on rare occasions are the requirements similar.)

Briner and Iannaccone (1966) compare the activities engaged in by principals and supervisors.   They write:

> The duties of the principal were characterized by words indicative of command functions such as: organizes, directs, supervises, exercises, administers, plans, allocates, and certifies; the supervisor provides, assists, participates, develops, plans, furnishes, and conducts, suggesting a more indirect influence (192-193).

> The nature of work regarding instruction was distinctive for each office.   The principal's office dealt mainly with a multiplicity of managerial tasks, which precluded working extensively with department chairmen and teachers on instructional matters interacting with teachers, department chairmen and principals (195).

Opportunity

The supervisory position provides an opportunity for the establishment of a career as a staff member in the central office of a school district.   The post may or may not be highly stable.   It may also be an advancement in the staff hierarchy.   A rare opportunity also exists for promotion into the deputy, associate, or assistant superintendency of instruction.   In general, however, the supervisory position provides lateral movement and a secure career at the central office.

The Elementary Principalship

There are a few women who do enter school administration in a similar manner as do white males.   They become elementary principals.   These women are more likely to obtain the position if they're situated in larger cities.

> Data compiled for 1971-72 by the National Council of Administrative Women in Education (NCAWE) for fourteen large cities (Atlanta, Boston, Chicago, Cincinnati, Cleveland, Denver, Los Angeles, New Orleans, New York City, Omaha, Portland, San Diego, San Francisco and Seattle) confirm this (NCAWE, 1973:9).   Altogether women filled 29.8 percent of the principalship positions of these cities.   Their strongest showing was at the level of the

elementary principalship, where they accounted for 36.5 percent of the total corps. In "middle" schools women accounted for only 13.9 percent of all principal positions. A still smaller proportion of high school principalships in the fourteen cities, 9.1 percent, were held by women (Meskin, 1978:325-326).

Obtaining the elementary principalship by women is much later than for white males. The Hemphill, Griffiths, and Frederickson (1962:66) study reports that in their sample of 232 elementary principals, 137 of them male and 95 of them women, the distribution of ages showed women to be approximately ten years older on the average than the men (Meskin, 331). Additionally, less than 10 percent of the men in the sample were single, whereas approximately 50 percent of the women were (Hemphill, et. al., 66; Meskin, 331). Gross and Trask (1976) report similar findings in their study. "About four-fifths of the sample of women were fifty years of age or older, but less than half of the men were; 63 percent of the women were single as compared to 5 percent of the men" (Meskin, 355).

As can be seen from the studies reported, women elementary principals are older than men and more likely to be single. These women are also different from those women found in specialist and supervisory positions.

Passage Through the Inclusion Boundaries

Permeability

Gross and Trask report on the difference between males and females in the manner by which the elementary principalship is acquired. They found that women principals had decided on a teaching career much earlier than the men, and teaching was the first career choice of 80 percent of them (as opposed to 46 percent of the men in the sample). Also, women first entertained the idea of becoming a principal at a far later age than men did, and, on the average, received their principalship many years after; for example, over twice the percentage of women as men in the sample were forty-six years of age or more when they first assumed the role of principal. Many men in the group of principals studied actively decided to seek the principalship for reasons related to occupational and social mobility and increase in income. Women, on the contrary, were frequently pushed into the principalship by "sponsors" who encouraged them professionally, or else they arrived there by a fortuitous accident (for example, by taking over the leadership role in a school during the illness of a regular principal). Once they became principals, women again showed less ambition to advance up the educational career ladder than men. They also seemed to find greater satisfaction in work related to instruction and to set a higher value on their ability to supervise instructional matters than male principals (Meskin, 1978:336).

A career portrait of the female principal emerges from their data. The woman principal begins her working years strongly committed to the occupation of teaching. Her eye is rarely on career advancement and she concentrates instead on knowing the ins and outs of her profession. When, often by a fluke, she is promoted to a principalship in later life, her long years as a basic service professional in an organization stand her in good stead. She shows greater ability and self-confidence in directing the instructional program than men do simply because of her deeper understanding of the art of teaching, and she also demonstrates a high degree of ability in administering the school, the milieu in which she worked so long. Because again she is not seeking promotion from her present rank, she commits herself wholeheartedly to the role of principal and is able to master the job in a highly competent fashion (Meskin, 336-337).

The data collected for this study which out of 350 administrators includes 127 women, indicate that women aspiring towards an administrative career cannot be as explicit about it as males. For example, the sample in this study shows that 55 out of the 127 (43.3 percent) women had wanted to be administrators before they entered teaching. The difference, then, between women and men is that women do not advance through the school hierarchy in the same way that men do.

How do women advance to an administrative position? If GASing, Getting the Attention of Superiors, is not acceptable for women, they must then look for other means. One means is to excel in teaching a particular area. For example, reading specialists get the attention of principals through their ability to teach reading The consequence, though, may be to become a specialist rather than a principal. Another means is to "just wait." One female principal stated:

I thought many times that I'd never be referred for a principalship. I did my job well. I stayed out of controversies. I supported the principal. My students scored high in math for three years straight. Everyone was nice but no one seemed to notice. I couldn't possibly let anyone know how badly I wanted some of the principalships that opened up. Finally, one day the principal said, "There's an elementary school on the other side of town whose principal is retiring. He asked me if I had anyone here who was a hard worker and a good person. I thought of you. Would you like to take over that school next year? I'll help you get acquainted with some of the work this year (January, 1976).

What we find is that the acquisition of an administrative position by a woman cannot be totally explained in terms of engaging in GASing behaviors. Women obtain their positions because they excel in some content area. They are asked to be specialists and they are likely to remain there. Those women who are asked to be principals are more likely to be asked fortuitously. Since they have displayed outstanding competence, a woman is considered for the position during an unforeseen occasion.

Two consequences result from this practice. The organizational members are not provided with a clearly legitimated reason for placing the woman in an administrative post. The second consequence is that women learn to behave in a passive manner regarding their career options. The first consequence serves to justify moves directed at removing women from administrative posts. The second serves to retain women in those positions most conducive to passivity such as the elementary principalship.

An example of one of the ways in which women adjust to the organizational environment expectations is explained in the Greabell and Olsen (1973) study. They tried to determine the areas in which females would prefer being involved in decision-making. The women selected curriculum and being consulted by the state legislature as areas they'd be involved in. The researchers view these areas as "safe choices." In contrast, the areas regarding the selection of entering teachers and tenure for both administrators and teaching personnel were rated much lower. The researchers contend these are risk areas which females avoid. This researcher would say that female teachers have "learned" in the institutional setting that they jeopardize their jobs if they express interest in certain areas. The same article repeats the concern that females aren't career oriented or upwardly mobile. This researcher contends that women learn that they cannot afford to express aspirations. Those women who are upwardly mobile learn to contain their desires and proceed to behave in particular ways to increase their chances for being "selected" at some point or being "around at a critical time."

Paloma and Garland (1971:538) refer to this type of adjustment as "domestication." They claim women have been socialized to tolerate domestication. Having to sustain multiplicity of roles due to marriage and family obligation, accepting less in the work world becomes tolerable as part of the whole package of women's roles.

Filtering Properties

There are two types of women found in educational administration: those who occupy the specialist, supervisory and elementary principalships and those who occupy the secondary principalships, associate, assistant and deputy superintendents and superintendencies. The specialists and supervisors and elementary principals have been presented. The second group will now be described.

Because men command the building site administrative positions as principals and the line positions at the central office with the attendant occupation of the superintendency, a structure is created which has severe consequences for those women who do obtain the secondary principalships and line positions of the central office.

Kanter (1977) presents an explanation of proportional representations of kinds of people:

> Skewed groups are those in which there is a preponderance of one type over another, up to a ratio of perhaps 85:15. The numerically dominant types also control the group and its culture in enough ways to be labeled "dominants." The few of another type in a skewed group can appropriately be called "tokens." (For) ...they are often treated as representatives of their category, as symbols, rather than individuals. If the absolute size of the skewed group is small, tokens can also be solos, the only one of their kind present, but even if there are two tokens in a skewed group, it is difficult for them to generate an alliance that can become powerful in the group (208).

Tokens

Women in educational administration find themselves in skewed groups if they enter the line positions. As members of a skewed group their quality of participation is distinct from that of white males and other females. Being tokens in this setting, their participation is conditioned in a certain way. As Kanter (1977) states, "Tokens get attention. One by one, they have higher visibility than dominants looked alone; they capture a larger awareness share" (210). They provide "contrast - polarization and exaggeration of differences" in order to fit the generalization regarding their type (211). They are famous within the school district. For example, female deputy superintendents were used as examples of how not be as women and as examples of the exaggerated "administrator" type. An instance is the following.

> A female teacher said, "I don't want to ever be an administrator. When I look at Dr. Denton and when I hear about her coldness and how bright she is, I know I'd never be happy being like that. She's not feminine at all" (December, 1976).

> Another male teacher said, "She's just like an administrator. She strides through our grounds. When she meets with us, she's so impersonal, businesslike and efficient. She dresses as if she's in some corporate meeting and her hairdo is always so severe" (December, 1976).

> One of her subordinates, a supervisor, said, "She's demanding; she wants perfection. She's too much! Of all the administrators in this district she's the ultimate. She's here early; she is always ready, and she leaves late.

Sometimes I feel she knows more about my work than I do" (December, 1976).

"Tokens perform their jobs under public and symbolic conditions from those of dominants" (Kanter, 1977:212). When female administrators err, it is widely publicized; it is the source of conversation for a lengthy period of time throughout the district. For example, an assistant superintendent approved a release of a report which had incomplete data. The report was later used as the basis for developing a program. Because some figures were not in the report to be used in calculating the cost, plans for the program were inaccurate. When it was discovered that the fault lay in the incomplete report, the assistant superintendent was severely criticized. That incident was used as an example for several years to warn personnel about making mistakes (February, 1975-79).

As "public figures" these women cannot display emotions. Kanter (1977) refers to this as projecting "public persona that hide inner feelings" (214). For example, an incident occurred during an administrators' meeting in which an issue was being hotly contested. Some principals wanted to provide smoking facilities in their schools and others did not. A female principal presented her opinion and in the course of the presentation, her voice rose and excitedly advocated a particular plan. During her presentation, the associate superintendent for personnel interrupted her and said, "Joyce, if you can't present your viewpoint calmly now, it might be best to wait until you can. We can't be too emotional about this" (March, 1977). Later, a group of principals, male and female, stated, "Everyone was emotional about the smoking item. Why was Joyce asked to be calmer?" (March, 1977). Therefore, successful administrative women are expected to be calm. Their public performance is more open to scrutiny.

Another common characteristic considered to be problematic for women is that they talk too much. One of the first things women are warned about is "to listen carefully, but keep quiet!" One newly appointed female supervisor said, "I hadn't been at my desk two hours before Dr. Harris came over to talk to me. His first point was, "You don't have time to visit here. You don't have time to repeat what you hear, and you don't have time to offer your analysis of situations. The thing to remember is to listen, to do, and remain silent" (March, 1979). A female secondary principal said when she was relating her first days on the job:

Just before we left for the executive meeting Dr. Brand called me to stop by his office. While there he said, "What we discuss in these meetings is confidential. The most important thing is not to repeat our meeting proceedings. For women, one of the first things they're tested on is to determine if they can keep secrets. Can you?" (November, 1977).

In summary, women are warned about being silent and keeping secrets.

The symbolic consequences for these women are likewise serious. Every act committed by the women tends to be evaluated beyond its meaning for the organization and taken as a sign of "how women perform." When treated as symbols or representatives, regardless of their expertise or interest, they are expected to present "the woman's point of view." Additionally, upper level women are "scrutinized by those on a lower level who discuss the merits of things done by the higher-ranking women and considered them to have implications for their own careers" (Kanter, 1977:215). The consequence is that business and personal decisions, then, "get handled by tokens with an awareness of their extended symbolic consequences" (216). An aspiring supervisor said, "I'll probably have to show Mr. Dexter that I am cooler and calmer than Miss David" (January, 1975).

The most serious professional consequence of the structure presented above is that tokens don't have to work hard to have their presence noticed, but they do have to work hard to have their achievements noticed (216). There is disproportionate "focus on appearance and other non-ability traits" (217). For example, in describing a recently appointed female associate superintendent, a principal said, "She's attractive, dresses smartly, wears her hair short and in its natural color, and above all is well proportioned" (March, 1976).

Another consequence mentioned by Kanter is that tokens must never make dominants look bad. One form of peer retaliation was "to abandon a successful woman the first time she encountered problems" (218). One of the newly appointed secondary principals had some parents complain about extra-curricular schedules. When the matter was brought up at a principal's meeting she was told to "fix up the schedule, straighten out the parents, or abandon ship." She changed the schedule several times only to be told at about mid-January that "It seems that directing a middle high school is too much for you. We believe being a supervisor is better suited to you" (August, 1978-February, 1979).

As tokens, women in educational administration respond in varying ways. One is to "over-achieve" and publicly perform in a manner to minimize organizational and peer concerns. These individuals are outstanding, exceptional and able to perform well under close observation. They have also developed skills in impressions management that permit them to retain control over the extra consequences loaded into their acts. They are able to maintain a delicate balance between always doing well and not generating peer resentment. The result of these exacting demands is that successful women are those slightly older than their male peers. In addition to their strong technical backgrounds they have also had extensive experience as token women among males. These are the women who may become superintendents. Kanter (1977) claims that the success of such women is most likely to increase the prospects for hiring more women in the future; they worked for themselves and as symbols (219).

Another means of responding is to accept notoriety and trade on it. This is the least likely to succeed because of the power of peers (Kanter, 1974:220). A third means is to become "socially invisible." These women try to minimize their sexual attributes; sometimes they adopt "mannish dress." These are the persons who avoid public events and occasions for performance. The consequence is that by using this strategy, the organization concludes that women are ineffective and low risk-takers. Practically, these women are the ones who are ultimately demoted. They are placed in undesirable organizational settings and forgotten until an occasion arises when the presence of women is important.

Why are women not accepted among line administrators? Kanter (1977) presents three reasons why tokens cannot become members of their organizational group. "First, a token represents the danger of challenge to the dominants' premises. (Second), the self-consciousness created by the token's presence is uncomfortable to people who prefer to operate in casual superficial, and easy going ways, without much psychological self-awareness. (Also), part of the hostility peer groups show to new kinds of people stems from uncertainty about their behavior" (222).

Tokens not only threaten but they may be "used" in organizational settings. Kanter states that tokens are causes for interruptions in gatherings. They are required to assure the dominants that their current exchange is acceptable. In order to insure inclusion in at least some functions, tokens are expected to demonstrate loyalty to their dominant peers. This takes several forms. There is pressure to turn against members of their own category. They can let slide statements prejudicial to other members of their category; they can allow themselves to be viewed as exceptions; they can be subjects of ridicule or joking remarks about their incompetence; or they can demonstrate their gratitude for being included by not criticizing their situation or pressing for any more advantages. "One major taboo area involved complaints about the job or requests for promotion" (220).

In brief, it is seen that "tokens, paradoxically, are the most relaxed and feel the most "natural" during the official parts of the business day when other people are the most constrained by formal roles" (239).

What we find, then, is a few women who are socialized in the company of males. This results in specific attitudes and behaviors. First, these women strongly resist admitting they've been discriminated against. They resist describing their careers and the manner by which they obtained their positions. In short, they become very cautious individuals.

Second, these women are highly achievement-oriented individuals. They personally set out to "prove" they can do something. Third, they are keenly aware of their support within the organization. Most of these women are strongly supported by a powerful organizational superior. The superior is usually a principal, superintendent, or a university professor. Fourth, these women are used to difficulties at each advancement level. In the present study all associate, deputy and assistant superintendents and superintendents could cite some example of resistance from the organization each time they were promoted. They learned to expect it, accept it, and be prepared to battle for their advancement. Fifth, women administrators are reluctant to express further aspirations. They speak in terms of "doing their best now." Furthermore, their co-workers could not cite instances in which these persons complained, asked for promotions, or expressed aspirations. The women were perceived as highly competent, exceptions, dependable and probably capable of being super-intendents. For example, one superintendent in describing a female associate superintendent stated:

> Jane has been the best thing for this district during this period. She has worked hard with the integration forces. She has helped develop a curriculum plan in bilingual education. She has helped to keep the morale of this school district high. I know she can be a successful superintendent, but I don't expect her to toot her own horn. I will do it for her (May, 1977).

This person is now superintendent. However, during the three years of interaction with her, she never once expressed desires for the position even though she did everything else which was required to obtain it.

Women, being unable to independently seek advancement must subtly allow superior males to advance them. Males, on the other hand, even though subject to the same mechanism were heard to loudly proclaim desires for the superintendency, to inform others they were applying for the positions and in general to alert others of their ambitions.

The most necessary ingredient in obtaining a line administrative position is a sponsor. Marshall (1979) states in her study:

> A person can qualify for an administrative staff position by obtaining special knowledge and experience through for-mal training. Curriculum directors, head counselors, (and) elementary principals can fill a position successfully when they acquire special education.

> Line positions in school administration, such as high school principals (and) assistant superintendent are middle and higher management positions. Formal training and technical expertise are not enough to make a person qualified. People who fill these positions must meet formal education requirements and informal requirements to be able to perform (83-84).

The informal training takes place in several ways, but the most intense part of it takes place within the sponsor-protege relationship.   It   not   only   provides   the   initial   push   into administration, but the explication of appropriate behaviors and attitudes, and access to line positions for task learning and promotion (85).   The serious problem for women in establishing this relationship is that most sponsors are likely to be male.   Because the sponsor-protege relationship is by nature ambiguous and because of the differential expectations between men and women, the establishment of a sponsor-protege relationship is problematic for women whereas it is not for men.   After a line administrative position is obtained, other problems arise for women in retaining their positions.   First, because of the prominance of males as school administrators   role   models   for   aspiring   women   are   absent. Therefore, women must learn to be administrators to a great degree on their own (Marshall, 1979:89-94).

Second, as token members in educational administration, women experience great isolation in the work setting.   Third, exclusion continues due to the prevalent practice of male administrators to engage in informal activities not acceptable to women.   Fourth, women are severely tested on male-oriented criteria.   Loyalty, willingness to compromise, perserverence in difficult situations, strength, ability to handle tough tasks, and ability to strike a proper balance of personal and career priorities must be established along with professional competence (94-105).

In brief, for women career socialization is much more severe than for men.   The primary reason for this is that only must women change due to the demands of the organizational setting, but also due to the cultural aspects of women.   Women have first of all been socialized as women in a culturally defined manner.   For those women who have been successfully socialized in this way, departing from this cutural norm is difficult at best.   Furthermore, since the organizational demands are based on a male orientation, cultural considerations related to women are minimal if not altogether absent.   Therefore,   women   are   required   to   change   in   two fundamental ways as they advance through the hierarchy.   They must change in regard to the culturally socialized woman and in regard to the demands placed by the new work setting.

As school administrators change organizationally and culturally the organization contributes in a number of ways.   As Spradley and Mann (1975) state in their study, the organization contains stress points created by the relationships between the actors.   In school administration, the stress points are: 1) the relationship between female   teachers   and   female   administrators;   2)   the   relationships between   male   teachers   and   female   administrators;   3)   the relationships between female staff administrators and female line administrators; 4) the relationships between male staff administrators and female line administrators; and 5) the relationship between male and female line administrators.

The stress is recorded in the manner by which school admi- nistrators are perceived.   Spence (1971) reports findings regarding male and female teachers' perceptions of male and female principals. In a comparison of scores assigned by male teachers, it was found that the male principals were scored higher on tolerance of uncertainty, and the female principals were scored higher on production emphasis. Those scores assigned by female teachers revealed more discriminating differences. Male principals were scored higher on six dimensions: reconciliation, tolerance of uncertainty, tolerance of freedom, consideration, predictive accuracy and integration. Female principals were perceived more positively on representation and production emphasis (2985A).

> More experienced, older teachers scored the female prin-
> cipal significantly higher on persuasiveness, predictive
> accuracy, and integration than did the less experienced,
> younger teachers. In addition, older teachers scored the
> female principal more positively on reconciliation, initiation
> of structure, consideration and superior orientation than
> did younger teachers (2985A).

In another study, Kobayashi (1974) found that female elementary principals are perceived differently than are male elementary principals. She reports that female principals were perceived as "exhibit(ing) greater concern with moving the organization toward its goals, with closer monitoring of teachers, and with being guided by rules and policies." Also, "staff of male principals perceived themselves as "going through the motions" of problem solving more than did the staffs of female principals" (130A).

Longstreth (1973) also, even though reporting few differences between male and female principals, did find that "males perceived female principals as either "subordinate-centered" or "boss-centered", and male principals as "boss-centered." Females perceived female principals as "subordinate-centered" and male principals as "boss-centered" (2224-A).

Not much is reported about perceptions concerning line and staff officers. However, since it's been shown in this study that the women who occupy these positions differ, it can be assumed that some stress is likely.

Lastly, the stress point between the female administrator and the male administrators is the most intense. Some anthropologists (Radcliffe-Brown, 1965) who have identified this stress have also reported that the form of the resolution of the conflict takes place within a "joking relationship" (90-91). This relationship is

> between two persons in which one is by custom permitted
> and in some instances, required to tease or to make fun of
> the other, who, in turn, is required to take no offense...
> (It) is a peculiar combination of friendliness and antagonism.
> The behavior is such that in any other social context it
> would express and arouse hostility; but is not meant
> seriously and must not be taken seriously. There is a
> pretense of hostility and a real friendliness. To put it
> another way, the relationship is one of permitted disrespect
> (89).

Spradley and Mann (1975) identify four basic characteristics to this relationship. First, "it is restricted to certain participants" (90). In school administration it is restricted to male and female school administrators. It is localized among the secondary principals and central office administrators, but it is common to see male secondary principals and central office administrators direct this relationship to recent or upwardly mobile elementary female administrators. A necessary ingredient in this exchange is that the female administrator must be willing to participate. As Mauss (1967:40) states, "Failure to give or to receive, like failure to make return gifts, means a loss of dignity." Also, "this joking relationship is complex, full of subtle nuances and informal rules that must be mastered if participation is to be culturally appropriate" (from Spradley and Mann, 1975:90). In school administration, this is particularly difficult because there is a distinction between those women who are elementary principals and those who have advanced to the secondary level and central office. What is seen is that established elementary female principals participate with ease. Those on the upward climb do not.

Spradley and Mann (1975) explain what contributes to ease in this joking relationship. They say, "It takes time to learn how to participate in joking with skill. This is true, in part, because a boundary exists between serious insults and joking comments that is not always clear (especially for recent position holders). (Also), even when joking, women must maintain a subordinate position, careful that their ritual insults do not denigrate a male (administrator)" (93).

In the present study, upwardly mobile female administrators refused to participate in joking. The only women who were seen to exchange jokes were younger newly appointed position holders, established older female elementary principals and a female superintendent. The greatest degree of ease in this exchange was seen displayed only by older female elementary principals. What is concluded about this joking behavior among school administrators is that upwardly mobile women refuse to participate; the men exchange humor among themselves and selected female types.

A second characteristic of the joking relationship is that "it is restricted to certain settings" (Spradley and Mann, 1975:90). This joking relationship is marked by a temporary suspension of the restraints that usually govern interaction.... The restrictions involved places... as well as times" (93). The "primary settings" for school administrators is just prior to formal meetings when people mill around waiting for the meetings to start or when they are waiting for someone to join them to go somewhere. Most often these settings are used to joke about "inadequate performances in the expected role" (94). The jokes may include males as well as females, but the intent of the joke is to point to the errors made while enacting the role. The most common subjects for these jokes are newly appointed administrators and women. The jokes may cover dress as well as interpersonal bungling or errors. What administrators learn early in their careers is that senior administrators may treat their errors in one of two ways: assist the newcomer, or turn the occasion into a joking insult (95). Women administrators learn that their failures are viewed not only in relation to their organizational position but also as women and the joking will reflect both aspects (95).   Women were never observed to exchange humor in a formal setting.

Another characteristic of the joking relationship between male and female school administrators is that "it involves ritual insults and sexual topics" (90).   For those in school administration, it appears that when the subject matter "centers on insults made in jest, when direct references to sexual behavior, and when comments about anatomical features with sexual meanings are used, the women are viewed as having obtained their positions illegitimately, and it is likely they won't be administrators very long.   The prominant characteristic is that only males engage in this sort of exchange. Every woman who was observed to "retort in kind" was rapidly demoted.   Therefore, one way of indicating the acceptance of the women among administrators is the use of this specific kind of subject matter.   Few women who were observed to be subjects of this type of joking continued as administrators.   This relationship therefore serves to maintain the male as superior.   In other words, school administrators could joke with females more freely concerning role inadequacy.   When sexual topics were raised, the only legitimate participants were males even though the victim of the joke was female.

The fourth characteristic of this joking relationship is that "it is a public encounter" (90).   "The joking behavior usually occurs in the presence of an audience who listen, observe, and vicariously enjoy the display".... (97-98).   Joking was observed to be inappropriate between a male and female administrator when alone. Because of the informality associated with the exchange of these jokes, the audience could include secretaries, and all other administrators.   Because the primary settings for these jokes were prior to meetings, teachers, parents, and students were not likely to be part of the audience.   Therefore, the audience usually consisted of other administrators and their secretaries.

The joking relationship served several functions.   It resolved structural conflict in the social structure of administrators.   It deflected feelings of inadequacy by the women administrators away from the relationship.   It provided a means for handling inadequate role performance.   It served to teach others about role performance.   Most importantly, it maintained the status inequality of female administrators and reinforced the masculine values pervasive in school administration.

What is seen, then, is that the exchange of humor, joking and witticisms remained under the control of senior male administrators. Upwardly mobile females adapted to this cultural norm by withdrawing from participation.   Those women who were not acceptable to the senior males were constant subjects until they resigned, left or were demoted to the classroom.   Established older elementary female principals reinforced the pervasive structure.

During the period of this study, out of the 127 women who were observed, 12 of them were observed to experience the use of joking to demote them. Eight were newly appointed administrators. Four had been administrators for varying lengths of time. One of the newly appointed administrators stated when she resigned:

> If I have to bear the brunt of everyone's jokes for the rest of the year in order to prove my worth, I'll explode. I've never been treated like this. I didn't ask for the job. They can have it back and I'll look for another one where I don't have to take everybody's dirty jokes (May, 1975).

A female administrator who'd just been appointed acting assistant principal of a junior high school was teased about the way she smoked her cigarette. She stood up at the table and retorted to the senior male, "Why you _____, what's it to you if I smoke this way? I don't care how you_____ or _____ so" Within the semester she was sent back to the classroom. Later she said, "I made a serious mistake taking on _____ (the senior school administrator) (October, 1978).

A female deputy superintendent told a newly appointed female elementary principal, "Don't place yourself in a position where you'll be teased about something. But if you are teased, take it and refuse to exchange remarks. The safest thing is to be unobtrusive" (December, 1976).

Another principal said, "I don't get it. How can Mrs. Pick joke with the superintendent and get away with it?" The associate superintendent for personnel responded, "She's been here a long time, she is his informant. She'll always be an elementary principal. Don't worry about it" (November, 1978).

An observation of female administrators indicates that they are inhibited in their personal behaviors. Upwardly mobile women were never observed to yawn, to stretch, to complain, or to engage in idle chatter. When male and female administrators interacted a specific behavioral norm was observed to persist for all. Newly appointed administrators were permitted some latitude in deviating from the regular norms. If they persisted they were removed from their positions. Successful women administrators protrayed a conservative female image. Senior administrators dictated the acceptable norms. The result was that successful mid-career women were severely constrained in their behavior. The relaxation of these requirements among women does not take place until the women achieve the superintendency.

An associate superintendent in describing her adjustment said, "I know I can't be like the male administrators. I know I can't be like the female teachers, so I've learned to adjust here, comply there, and remain wary. Sometimes, I think it isn't fair, but most of the time, I just think about doing and keeping my job" (March, 1977).

Formal settings provided the most predictable and stable contexts for behaving properly. Women are able to adapt to this more readily and adeptly. The pervasive norm is that women take a secondary role to men in conducting the school business. On occasions when a particular issue is raised by a woman which has powerful merit, a woman may assume a prominant role, but this is temporary and limited to that issue only. If the woman has a reputation of being particularly astute, has seniority in the group, and is liked, the woman may command total responsibility for the issue. Those women who haven't established themselves, who appear vulnerable for one reason or another may have their ideas "stolen" from them by a male.

For example, a newly appointed female associate superintendent prepared a work flow chart for the evaluation of personnel in the district. The chart was accepted by the group, but by the second session in dealing with the administration of the work flow, a male director was claiming ownership of the chart and by the third he was directing the discussion and planning the total evaluation program.

A similar incident occurred in another district, but in this case the woman had been in the district for several years, had shown competence many other times, and when a male administrator tried to claim ownership of a plan, the rest of the administrators reminded him that Dr. Amelia Jones had presented the plan. No one attempted to take over her plan after that.

In general, however, women are not as active in formal settings as men. Women are less likely to be successful in informal settings. Many women choose to simply not participate in informal gatherings. Other women attend but they play a very minor role in the gatherings. Few women successfully interact and participate in them.

One striking example of the type of participation that takes place on an informal basis is the exchange of work experience. White males enthusiastically relate their "war stories" as they've come up the ranks. The stories are embellished with descriptions of problems, the participants, the newness of the problem, and finally the heroic solution. Each white male tries to outdo the other in terms of quantity, severity and complexity of problems. They seek each other out for these exchanges and they relate to each other in terms of sharing these known "stories" with others in the field.

Meantime, women listen to these stories, approve and may on occasion ask a question, but a woman is not expected to have "war stories" of her own. If a female administrator attempts to relate a story, she is ignored, interrupted and in general it is immediately made known that no one is interested. Those women who have "been around" in these circles don't even volunteer any remarks that might invite a story. During the period in which data for this study were collected, not once was a woman observed to relate a complete "war story" among the other administrators. Newcomers were observed to attempt to relate some "story". They were also observed to be restrained. One associate superintendent said, "No one is interested in our stories. No one believes we have the same experiences. But the critical point is that no one wants to hear a woman has been a heroine" (April, 1978).

An important point to this is that if it is going to be known that women have done something outstanding, it is related by others, usually the superintendent. One female high school principal said:

> The riot was over, the papers had not blown up the incident. The school had not closed and I was able to go about my work as usual. It was the only school in the district that was this stable. I could and would not dare mention this to anyone. The only one who made the comparison, who gave me credit for my work, was the superintendent. I have never been able to tell anyone how I accomplished that. No one has asked me how I did it (November, 1978).

When a central office official was asked about the performance of the above mentioned principal, he said, "She's quite a remarkable person. Her successes have been fortuitous and she runs one of the best schools. Other principals are as good as she is, but not as lucky" (November, 1978).

In conclusion, women who wish to establish careers must change regarding the cultural expectations for women. At the same time, however, they must behave under certain conditions as women. The second change which is necessary is that they must change their perspectives as organizational participants in the same way that white males do. As principals they must consider adults, management and their school as the focal centers. As central office assistant, associate, and deputy superintendents they must consider the school district's policies and ultimately integrate their personal needs into the organizational demands.

Those who are successful are those women who view themselves professionally, who have had much experience working with men, and who are personally motivated to be successful in these types of settings.

The most severe barriers for women are: 1) the initial departure from teaching; 2) occupying those positions which don't provide opportunities for upward mobility such as the elementary principalships; 3) losing out to white males in the competition for line positions; and 4) coming up the wrong career path, as for example, being a specialist rather than a principal.

NOTES

[1]The Scriven and Nunnery (1974) study does not make a distinction between central office based specialists and other supervisors.

CHAPTER 5

Minorities in Educational Administration

INTRODUCTION

It has been seen how admission into educational administration is gained through teaching. This is because teaching is the entry level position for most certificated school personnel. The one exception to this is in the case of minorities.

There are two groups of minorities within the school system. Those who entered before the mid-sixties and early seventies and those who entered during and after. Those who entered before the mid-sixties began teaching and possessed regular credentials as did all others. Those who entered the school district during the mid-sixties and seventies may have started in another capacity besides teaching. Many entered without teaching credentials or any of the usual requirements for certificated teachers. They came in as counselors and teacher aides. Training and experience opportunities were provided so that in time these persons could earn regular teaching credentials. Many chose to do so.

Where are minorities located in school districts? First, detailed records and statistics of minorities on school district staffs are not readily available. Second, an overview of the literature shows that very few minorities are actually employed by school districts. The Equal Employment Opportunity Commission (1977)[1] reports that the total United States (7,248 school districts and 69,439 schools) full-time staff in 1975 was 3,590,411. Of these, 1,273,905 (35.5%) were male, 2,317,306 (64.5%) were female, 3,001,134 (83.6%) were white, and 589,277 (16.4%) were minority. Of these 461,486 (12.9%) were Black, 99,523 (2.8%) were Hispanic, 15,496 (.4%) were Asian, and 12,772 (.4%) were American Indian.

The school positions were categorized in several levels. A few are listed below to provide a description of the distribution of minorities. The total employment of officials, administrators/managers or central office personnel was 43,208. Of these, 36,690 (84.9%) were male, 6,518 (15.1%) were female, 39,853 (92.2%) were white, and 3,355 (7.8%) were minority. Of these, 2,349 (5.5%) were Black, 767 (1.8%) were Hispanic, 77 (.2%) were Asian, and 162 (.4%) were American Indian.

Out of a total of 72,285 principals 63,015 (87.2%) were male, 9,270 (12.8%) were female, 65,208 (90.2%) were white, and 7,077

(9.7%) were minority.   Of these, 5,784 (8.0%) were Black, 948 (1.3%) were Hispanic, 108 (.1%) were Asian and 237 (.3%) were American Indian.

Out of 30,691 non-teaching assistant principals (vice-principles), 24,528 (79.9%) were male, 6,163 (20.1%) were female, 25,005 (81.5%) were white, and 5,686 (18.5%) were minority.   Of these, 4,803 (15.6%) were Black, 658 (2.2%) were Hispanic, 125 (.4%) were Asian and 100 (.4%) were American Indian.

Out of 1,004,641 elementary teachers, 168,258 (16.7%) were male, 836,383 (83.3%) were female, 865,430 (86.2%) were white, and 139,211 (13.9%) were minority.   Of these 113,848 (11.3%) were Black, 17,244 (1.7%) were Hispanic, 5,646 (.6%) were Asian and 2,473 (.3%) were American Indian.

Out of 902,103 secondary teachers, 488,401 (54.1%) were male, 413,702 (45.9%) were female, 808,149 (89.6%) were white and 93,944 (10.4%) were minority.   Of these 74,769 (8.3%) were Black, 13,692 (1.5%) were Hispanic, 3,345 (.4%) were Asian and 2,138 (.2%) were American Indian.

Out of 26,385 consultants and supervisors of instruction, 12,782 (48.4%) were male, 13,603 (51.6%) were female, 22,495 (85.2%) were white, and 3,890 (14.7%) were minority.   Of these 3,081 (11.7%) were Black, 625 (2.3%) were Hispanic, 68 (.2%) were Asian and 116 (.5%) were American Indian.

In California, out of 477 school districts which included 6,398 schools the reports shows the following.   Out of 317,570 staff, 127,943 (40.3%) were male, 189,627 (59.7%) were female, 255,017 (80.3%) were white, and 62,553 (19.7%) were minority.   Of these, 26,397 (8.3%) were Black, 25,059 (7.9%) were Hispanic, 9,182 (2.9%) were Asian and 1,915 (.6%) were American Indian.

Out of 3,985 officials, administrators, managers or central office executive positions, 3,317 (82.2%) were male, 668 (16.8%) were female, 3,558 (89.3%) were white, and 427 (10.8%) were minority.   Of these, 163 (4.1%) were Black, 200 (5.0%) were Hispanic, 37 (1.0%) were Asian, and 27 (.7%) were American Indian.

Out of 6,350 principals, 5,438 (85.6%) were male, 912 (14.4%) were female and 5,684 (89.5%) were white, and 666 (10.5%) were minority.   Of these, 307 (4.9%) were Black, 234 (3.8%) were Hispanic, 79 (1.2%) were Asian and 43 (.7%) were American Indian.

Out of 4,038 non-teaching assistant principals (vice-principals), 2,447 (60.6%) were male, 1,591 (39.4%) were female, 3,351 (83.0%) were white, and 687 (17.0%) were minority.   Of these, 339 (8.4%) were Black, 234 (5.8%) were Hispanic, 85 (2.1%) were Asian and 29 (.7%) were American Indian.

Out of 95,239 elementary teachers, 20,372 (21.4%) were male, 74,867 (78.6%) were female, 81,021 (85.0%) were white, and 14,218 (15.0%) were minority.   Of these, 6,204 (6.6%) were Black, 4,010 (4.2%) were Hispanic, 3,534 (3.8%) were Asian, and 470 (.5%) were American Indian.

Out of 73,064 secondary teachers, 44,373 (60.7%) were male, 28,691 (34.4%) were female, 63,630 (87.1%) were white, and 9,434 (12.9%) were minority.   Of these, 3,780 (5.1%) were Black, 3,281

(4.5%) were Hispanic, 1,878 (2.6%) were Asian and 495 (.7%) were American Indian.

Out of 1,434 consultants and supervisors of instruction 705 (49.2%) were male, 729 (50.8%) were female, 1,217 (84.8%) were white, and 217 (15.1%) were minority.   Of these 78 (5.7%) were Black, 106 (7.4%) were Hispanic, 29 (2.0%) were Asian and 4 (.3%) were American Indian.   Table 6 shows the detailed representations.

An investigation of a particular minority group shows the consistency of minority participation in schools. For example, Casso (1975) reports that Mexican-Americans[2] are grossly underrepresented among teachers.   Of approximately 325,000 teachers in the Southwest, only about 12,000 or four percent are Mexican-American while about seventeen percent of the enrollment is Mexican-American.   Principals are also underrepresented.   Of approximately 12,000 school principals in the Southwest, less than 400 or three percent are Mexican-American.

The placement of Mexican-Americans in other positions such as assistant principals, counselors and librarians is similar to that of Mexican-American teachers and principals.   The same is true of the superintendency.   What is indicated is that Mexican-Americans are employed to a greater extent as teachers' aides or as non-professionals, especially custodians, rather than as professionals.

It has been seen that minorities participate in educational organizations in very small numbers.   Beyond that, minorities are situated in particular types of places.   An explanation of this difference between minorities and others is presented by Young (1973).   He cites three basic factors in the development and maintenance of ethnic and racial inferior group status.   They are: the visibility of members, the attributed competitive threat, and the extra situational derivative denigrating beliefs" (Young, 1973:1107).

These factors create a situation which contributes to not only limiting the numbers of those who participate but also where and how.   This results in a continuing relegated minority status.   A look at the participation of Mexican-Americans in schools shows the manner by which this status is actualized.   First, minorities are placed in particular types of schools.   For example, the United States Commission on Civil Rights[3] reported in 1971 that Mexican-American teachers are severely restricted in their school assignments.   More than one-half (55%) of all Mexican-American teachers in the Southwest teach in predominantly Mexican-American Schools.   One-third are in schools that are nearly all Mexican-American.

Also, "overall, Mexican-American principals are even more likely than either pupils or classroom teachers to be assigned to predominantly Mexican-American schools.   Nearly 65% of the Mexican-American principals head predominantly Mexican-American schools.   By comparison, 55 percent of the teachers and 45 percent of the pupils are in such schools.   More than two-fifths of all Mexican-American principals are in schools that are nearly all Mexican-American" (47).

The employment and assignment of Mexican-Americans in non-

TABLE 6. Public School Personnel Placement* 1975

	Male	Female	White	Minority	Black	Hispanic	Asian	Indian
Full-time Staff	1,273,905 35.5%	2,317,306 64.5%	3,001,134 83.6%	589,277 16.4%	461,486 12.9%	99,253 2.8%	15,496 .4%	12,772 .4%
Elementary Teachers	168,258 16.7	836,383 83.3	865,430 86.2	139,211 13.9	113,848 11.3	17,244 1.7	5,646 .6	2,473 .3
Secondary Teachers	488,401 54.1	413,702 45.9	808,149 89.6	93,944 10.4	74,769 8.3	13,692 1.5	3,345 .4	2,138 .2
Vice-principals	24,528 79.9	6,163 20.1	25,005 81.5	5,686 18.5	4,803 15.6	658 2.2	125 .4	100 .4
Principals	63,015 87.2	9,270 12.8	65,208 90.2	7,077 9.7	5,784 8.0	948 1.3	108 .1	237 .3
Consultants & Supervisors	12,782 48.4	13,603 51.6	22,495 85.2	3,890 14.7	3,081 11.7	625 2.3	68 .2	116 .5
Central Office Executive Positions	36,690 84.9	6,518 15.1	39,853 92.2	3,355 7.8	2,349 5.5	767 1.8	77 .2	162 .4
Full-time Staff	127,943 40.3	189,627 59.7	255,017 80.3	62,553 19.7	26,397 8.3	25,059 7.9	9,182 2.9	1,915 .6
Elementary Teachers	20,372 21.4	74,867 78.6	81,021 85.0	14,218 15.0	6,204 6.6	4,010 4.2	3,534 3.8	470 .5
Secondary Teachers	44,373 60.7	28,691 34.3	63,630 87.1	9,434 12.9	8,780 5.1	3,281 4.5	1,878 2.6	495 .7
Vice-principals	2,447 60.6	1,591 39.4	3,351 83.0	687 17.0	339 8.4	234 5.8	85 2.1	29 .7
Principals	5,438 85.6	912 14.4	5,684 89.5	666 10.5	307 4.9	234 3.8	79 1.2	43 .7
Consultants & Supervisors	705 49.2	712 50.8	1,217 84.8	217 15.1	78 5.4	106 7.4	29 2.0	4 .7
Central Office Executive Positions	3,317 82.2	668 16.8	3,558 89.3	427 10.8	163 4.1	200 5.0	37 1.0	27 .7

teaching professional positions resembles that of Mexican-American teachers. Very few hold these positions and many who do are assigned to schools that have a large Mexican-American enrollment. Mexican-Americans are more likely to be found in non-professional positions than in others. Of all school staff posts, Mexican-Americans constitute the largest proportion of those employed as teachers' aides (U.S. Commission on Civil Rights, 1971:47-48).

Except for counselors, the majority of Mexican-American non-teaching professionals are assigned to predominantly Mexican-American schools. There is a rather even distribution of the Mexican-American counselors regardless of school composition. A much larger proportion of the other Mexican-American non-teaching professionals, such as assistant principals and librarians is concentrated in schools that are 75 percent or more Mexican-American (49).

However, regardless of the pattern of school assignment in all professional non-teaching positions, Mexican-Americans are most highly visible in schools that are 75 percent or more Mexican-American. Generally, the greater the Mexican-American composition of the enrollment, the greater the proportion of Mexican-Americans on the professional staff. Nevertheless, even in schools that are 75 percent or more Mexican-American, they constitute only a minority of the schools' staff (49-50).

Comparatively few Mexican-Americans are employed among the professional personnel at the district level. Only about 480 or 7 percent of more than 6,750 professionals in the survey area are Mexican-Americans. About 50 of the 480 are superintendents and associate or assistant superintendents. Nearly 55% of the Mexican-Americans holding these top district positions are employed in New Mexico (53).

Mexican-Americans form a smaller part of total district professional staff than they do of enrollment. Throughout the Southwest, proportionately four times as many students as district level professionals are Mexican-American. Generally, persons of this ethnic group make up a larger proportion of the work force in the positions of social worker, attendance officer, federal programs director, and community relations specialist than they do of other district level staff positions (53). About 75 percent of Mexican-American community relations specialists are employed by California School systems (U.S. Commission on Civil Rights, 1971:53).

Nearly half of the Mexican-Americans in the survey who hold professional positions in district offices are employed by school districts that are predominantly Mexican-American (53).

Second, as stated before, there are very few of them. For example, "even in schools that are predominantly Mexican-American, teachers of this ethnic background make up less than one-third of the total teaching staff. The low representation of Mexican-American teachers even in predominantly Mexican-American schools where they are concentrated underscores the paucity of Mexican-Americans employed as classroom teachers in the Southwest"

(44).

As with classroom teachers, the percentage of Mexican-American principals is also far below the proportion of Mexican-American pupils. While 17 percent of all pupils in the Southwest are Mexican-American only about 3 percent of the principals are of this ethnic background (45).

Third, as indicated previously, minorities may have entered the school organization in a non-traditional manner which displaces them in relation to the majority group. Additionally, tenure may not be granted to them at the end of their third year of teaching as readily as to others.

Fourth, gaining access to the school organization does not mean they have access to all positions. What occurs is that minorities are placed in posts not fully accepted by the school organization. For example, minority teachers are placed in foreign language, physical education, vocational education, bilingual education and other non-traditional subjects as well as in classes with high enrollments of minority students.

Fifth, if they are initially placed in a traditional curricular area, there is an overt attempt later on to relegate them to the lesser content and service areas. For example, a Hispanic woman was originally hired as a music teacher, but was advised during the second year to transfer to teach Spanish or bilingual education or acquiring tenure would be jeopardized. She refused and her contract was terminated.

Those minorities entering the school district in a non-teaching capacity are hired for the expressed reason to aid in solving school social problems dealing with their particular minority groups. For example, a Black male was hired during the mid-sixties' Watts riots and was told to "go to that junior high school and turn those kids around. We are paying you a good salary for one so young. You will have your own office, telephone and secretarial services. You see to it those students don't destroy _____ Junior High School" (May, 1978).

Being hired in this manner creates the expectation that these persons will not remain in their positions long. This is particularly true if the community becomes involved in the hiring process. For example, a Black area administrator was hired by the school district with community representatives. He was told, "You have been given an important position. We know you can relate to the kids and the community. All we ask is that you improve relations between them and us" (April, 1977). These minority persons are usually well educated but seldom do they possess state teacher or administrative credentials.

Those minority persons already located in school districts prior to the mid-sixties and early seventies may have been given administrative posts, but on most occasions if those positions were acquired during that period, they were clearly granted to calm the social unrest. This differs from being promoted as a reward for competence and prior accomplishments.

In rare cases, minorities have obtained administrative posts in the traditional manner.   Even so, in some cases, these persons experienced stress and on occasion lost their positions during the mid-sixties and seventies era.

Finally, the combination of all of these factors leads to the creation of a sub-structure within the school which is separate from the parent institution.

PASSAGE THROUGH THE HIERARCHICAL BOUNDARY
Permeability

When minorities enter teaching, they enter the elementary schools, physical education, Spanish and ethnic studies in greater numbers than in other areas.   In general, they tend to be located in the least desirable schools.   For example, Becker (1952) reports that the Chicago teachers start out in the most undesirable schools, but through time they move out to the more desirable ones.   He describes two major careers which are developed among the teachers.

The first type consisted of those teachers who attempted to move to a better school in a better neighborhood.   Several factors contributed to the success of the move – namely having knowledge about the good schools, not being of an ethnic type, or having a personal reputation that would cause the principal to informally reject the candidate, and being patient enough to wait for the transfer to the right school to take place.

The second type of career was characterized by a permanent adjustment to the "slum" school situation.   These careers were the result of the process of adjustment to the particular work situation to such an extent that the teacher was tied to a school otherwise considered undesirable.

Minorities being of an ethnic type do not leave the undesirable schools; instead they follow the second career described.   There are several ways by which these expectations are reinforced.   First, these teachers are described as "natively gifted" to teach the special student population.   Second, as already seen, if a minority enters teaching through an area not normally taught by a minority, as for example, music, chemistry or mathematics, these teachers are encouraged to pick up classes to teach "their own".   For example, Blacks are asked to teach Black culture or Black history.   In the case of Hispanics, they are encouraged to go into bilingual education and Spanish.   Those teachers who refuse to teach in these areas may not receive tenure.   The result is that minorities with tenure are found teaching minority students and classes.   To illustrate, a Hispanic administrator said:

> When I began teaching, I started with all math classes. You see, no one was certain about my ethnic origin. After about a year, it was suggested I pick up a Spanish class to help out. I did. At the beginning of the third year, half of

my classes were Spanish and half in math. When I commented, the principal said, "But you are talented in Spanish. I think you're a good teacher and I'd like you to get tenure in our district." I continued teaching Spanish and general math. I never got the advanced classes back! (January, 1978).

The consequence for the minority position holder is that for those who entered as non-teachers, their careers are limited to the position they occupy.

Those who enter teaching may have their careers terminated, altered or at least disrupted. The most successful way for minorities to obtain tenure, the first indication of organizational acceptance, is to accept an assignment that includes something associated with the ethnicity of the person. For example, Hispanic high school Spanish teachers are not likely to be challenged during the acquisition of tenure. This means that most minority teachers are to be found in areas which have some connection to their ethnicity.

Role Models

The explanation for the presence of minorities in particular content areas and schools offered by the organization is that these persons provide models for students to emulate and hopefully these attitudes will be reflected in their behavior. The perception is that minorities must be visible to their minority group, control them and thereby improve the organization's conditions. This results in certain consequences.

Administrators, or those potentially able to advance a minority person do not focus on the person. Their primary focus is on the students they deal with. This means that in order for minority persons to be at least positively viewed, they must contain the minority students. In this case, the administrator (principal) can proceed with the regular school business. This results in principals who know the minority person, know about them (in relation to their containment of the students) and tolerate them. They are described such as in the following:

Oh, yes, Mrs. Garcia. She's our bilingual teacher. We don't have many non-English-speaking students, so we don't need more than one teacher. I think she's effective. The students have been quiet and I haven't seen them or the teacher in a couple of weeks. You see, her classroom is that portable at the end of the campus (April, 1978).

Minority teachers are therefore expected to be role models to students of their own ethnic group. Also, other school personnel perceive them as ethnic teachers rather than as subject or grade level instructors. This, as Charters (1964) points out, would tend to limit minority teachers from interacting with others. This is so because a fundamental social structure among teachers is based on subject and grade level assignment.

Organizational Space
Working Environment

Minorities accept teaching positions in bilingual education, Black English, continuation school, Spanish, physical education, and other subject areas associated with the above. These subject areas have certain things in common. First, they're of low prestige, they draw "hard-to-teach, loud students", and they are controversial. For this reason, classrooms in which these teachers are located tend to be temporary buildings, portable trailers, or are otherwise inaccessible. These persons are far from the principal, far from the main arteries of campus travel and as far away from as many teachers as possible. Moreover, since the school itself, is likely to be the, or one of the dreariest in the school district, minorities are placed in undesirable schools. But beyond that, they are also set apart within that school.

The most direct consequence is that minority persons begin their professional socialization in a working environment that is unpleasant, depressing, lonely and confined to their ethnic group.

Interpersonal Relationships

It is clear to see that minority persons do not have opportunities to develop relationships with other professionals if they are placed as teachers in an environment as described above. Realizing that teaching is a solo occupation (Lortie, 1975) anyway, teaching becomes even more so for those minorities who are placed in classrooms not readily accessible, or far from the offices and teachers' working areas. This leads to the development of certain perspectives among teachers about their minority colleagues. This was described in several ways by school people. For example, one teacher said, "We like Maria very much. She's so shy, though. We hardly ever see her. I suppose we don't invite her because we feel she's different from us" (December, 1977). Another teacher describing a Black physical education teacher said, "She's tough. I'm almost afraid to speak to her. She's so loud. She dresses so casually. I'm not like that. But at least she keeps those Black kids in line" (February, 1977).

A principal commented about his group of bilingual teachers. "I had to schedule different lunch and break periods for them because the rest of the teachers complained they spoke Spanish in the teachers' lounge" (November, 1976).

The point is that minority teachers are highly constrained in their opportunities to develop interpersonal relationships with their co-workers due to their placement in teaching. This is true to a greater degree regarding establishing relationships with principals. Since their classrooms are usually far away from the principal's office, regular interaction is impossible. As long as the principal doesn't receive complaints, trips to the minority teacher's classrooms are not taken. Therefore, minorities do not develop intensive or extensive interpersonal relationships with the regular teaching staff or superiors.

Activities

Because minorities are hired in such specific areas, their activities are limited to specified students and curricular content. Moreover, since their working location is so secluded, the result is that minorities spend most of their working time helping the particular students who go to them. This is extended to cover lunch and recess periods. In most cases, this is welcomed by the rest of the staff. Because a number of those students detained by the minority teacher are likely to create problems elsewhere, the staff is relieved to know someone else has them. There is another consequence; the minority person becomes known as a different kind of teacher from the others. A student described one of the Black continuation school teachers thusly, "Mrs. Peterson was here last year, but she was better with those students who misbehaved, so I guess that's why she was transferred to the continuation school" (December, 1977).

A bilingual teacher was described by another student as "Mrs. Morales? Let's see, she's the one who teaches the Mexicans" (February, 1978). Minority teachers are thus constrained to very specific activities and this in turn creates an organizational expectation which further inhibits their participation. What is seen is that minorities' opportunities are severely curtailed due to the initial occupational placement and the activities in which they are engaged.

Special Projects Administrator

The issue of aspirations for minorities is a very real one. For example, as Mussen, et al. (1963) state:

> Aspirations are the individual's conception of the role in the social order which they would find most satisfactory. One thing minority individuals are practically certain to have in common is awareness of their special social status. This they learn early in life and are reminded of as long as they live (409).

Minorities either must restrict aspirations in accordance with ascribed roles, or suffer the uncertainties of attempting to overcome the majority concept of their proper place in society. There is also the possibility that fellow minority members may not approve of their aspirations because of conflict with group goals and standards. Further, success in the milieu of the dominant majority may be viewed as contempt or desertion by militant and less successful minority individuals.   Broadly generalized, the variety and inconsistencies of role expectations for minority individuals is a cause of role strain and makes the choice and accomplishment of personal objectives especially troublesome (Young, 1973:1117).

The above is actualized in educational administration in the creation of a sub-structure which separates minorities from others. Therefore, advancement for minorities means advancement within their own structure.   But even so, the organizational perspective is that minorities do not wish to advance organizationally.

In this sense, two socialization problems are posed for minorities.   The first is associated with the restricted environment, i.e., minorities are not placed in the regular school organization positions, but rather in those which contain students and others of their ethnic group.   The second is linked to the incongruency between the expectations arising from an occupational role and their placement.   The tendency has been to infer a connection between the community and the organization as long as minorities are hired by school districts.   This has resulted in creating organizational structures which are presumed to link the schools with the community.   Minorities are subsequently placed there.   In regard to minority advancement, these structures serve to restrain minority competition among minorities in minority positions.   Advancement for minorities is then independent of advancement for others.   The institutionalization of this process takes place in special projects administration.

Hierarchy

Special projects administration is composed of those responsible for programs normally externally supported to provide special aid and services to particular student groups.   Minority students are primary targets.   Within special projects, many positions of varying titles and responsibilities are created to carry out the mandates of the numerous programs.

The positions are to serve one general purpose and that is to administer the programs created for special groups of students. For example, a bilingual education director may be in charge of all of the bilingual programs in the school district.   Other assistant administrator positions may be created below that post which conduct in-service training, coordinate curricular offerings, and/or personnel.   Because there are a number of these positions available within a school district it is uncertain about where a particular position may be located hierarchically.   However, there are a few characteristics about these posts which aid in determining their structural placement.

If the position is one in which the office holder is housed in a school site, it can be assumed that the position is equal to or above that of teacher.   If the position-holder does a lot of teaching and little managing and if the principal is responsible for the person's evaluation, the person's post is likely to be equal to that of teacher. If the person is in charge of several schools and programs and is evaluated by a supervisor in the central office, even though housed at the school site, the position is hierarchically slightly above that of teacher but below that of principal.

If the position is housed at the central office and the person is evaluated by a central office position-holder, then that post is decidedly above that of teachers. It may be equivalent to that of principal. If the position is titled director, rather than assistant administrator, coordinator; specialist or supervisor, the position is likely to be equivalent to or above that of principal.

As stated before, minorities are placed in organizational positions which are separate from the parent organization. One reason is because these programs exist through the funding provided by external agencies. The positions are dependent on those special funds and therefore, they have to be granted on a, more or less, temporary basis. In other words, moving from teaching to special projects is not the same as advancing from teaching to the principalship.

There are several reasons for this. First, the assumption of a special projects position is not viewed as a promotional move or as a reward granted for outstanding accomplishments. It is viewed as filling a post by someone who has "native ability" and may be better than the other minorities. Second, the position will last only as long as funds for the position are available. The position of the principalship is necessary for the organization of schools and it is not likely that it will disappear. Furthermore, a career can be established within the position such as in the case of the elementary principalship. Beyond that, the principalship is a position which affords extraordinary opportunities for further advancement. Most special projects posts cannot provide any of these advantages.

In conclusion, the positions created by special funds are temporary regardless of their hierarchical placement. The greatest benefits they can provide are immediate, such as salary, experience, and title. They cannot insure careers for minorities.

One of the offices which is created by external funding serves as a link between the school district and the ethnic community. Sometimes it is titled area administrator. Its purpose is to maintain harmonious relationships between the community and the school. It is not acquired as a promotion but as a contractual assignment. For example, Ravitch (1974) reports that "local school boards hired their own district superintendents (area administrators) on a contractual rather than a tenured basis" (398). The consequence of this practice is that the position is not a secure one and it is not to be treated as a regular promotional move. Its hierarchical placement is ambiguous.

Organizational Space

Working Environment

As was stated previously, special projects posts house the occupant either at the school site or at the central office. At the school site, if the person is confined to the school, the working environment may not differ from that of teachers. However, if the position holder is responsible for several teachers in several schools throughout the district, the working space may resemble that of an administrator rather than a teacher. For example, an office with a telephone rather than a classroom would serve as the working area for the occupant.

Being housed at the central office does mean some fundamental changes from teaching. The occupant is located in an office instead of a classroom, with a telephone, clerical, and secretarial services available. Depending on the position, the office space may be shared or private. For example, directors are likely to have private offices, secretaries and telephone service. This placement may be alongside other supervisors and school adminsitrators. The rest of the position holders may be grouped together within a large unit of special projects.

The working environment for the area administrator is modest. It is usually located where it is the most accessible to his/her constituencies. In this case, it is not uncommon to find the office located at a high school. In smaller districts, it may be located at the central office. The most pronounced characteristics of this office are that they must appeal to the ethnic community. Therefore, the office decor may be ethnic, sparse, or neutral. Because community people are expected to frequent the office it is a place that is accessible to them but invisible to the decision-makers. Therefore, this work place is usually located on the first floor and somehow separated from the rest of the central office personnel; for example, it may be at the end of a long hall.

Interpersonal Relationships

The fundamental difference between special projects administrators and teachers is that they deal with adults. Because they are working with minority concerns, they generally deal with other minorities. The exception is if the position-holder is the only one housed at the school site who works with minority students. In that case, the interaction with adults may be minimal.

If the person is in charge of several schools and teachers, there are expanded opportunities for interactions, especially with other minorities. In the case of the area administrator, the significant others are community persons. This means that there are limited opportunities for interaction with school officials and school board members. Most important, they have little influence among teachers and principals because their major group of interest is the community. In sum, the opportunity for the development of intensive and extensive interpersonal relationships among the school organization's participants is slight.

If the person is located at the central office, the interaction may expand to non-minority adults. There are several features which contribute to this. To the extent that not all minorities are placed within the same working area, interaction with non-minorities will increase. To the extent that the position requires dialogue with the associate superintendents, superintendent and school board members, interaction with non-minorities will increase.

The position which contains this characteristic to the greatest degree is the directorship. Because the school district's responsibility for these programs is lodged in the director, he needs to maintain a constant relationship with the superintendent, his associates, and the school board. This provides for the development of intensive and extensive interpersonal relationships within the organization.

Activities

Several types of special projects administrators have been identified. Those who are located at the school and whose responsibilities are within the school engage in activities confined to students and instruction.

Those who are located at the school site but whose responsibilities extend to other schools and teachers, engage in more varied activities. They may instruct students, conduct workshops and in-service training for teachers and teacher aides. But the fundamental change is that they have added administrator and managerial duties to their work load. They prepare reports, coordinate programs, order materials and equipment, construct schedules, and increase their interaction with adults.

Area administrators, on the other hand, interact heavily with community persons. They attend community functions, speak at community gatherings, listen to community members' concerns and in general serve as school district representatives. They do not, however, normally speak for the school district. The data for the present study indicate that those who forget this are severely sanctioned by the superintendent and his associates and the school board.

Thus, the one group, which is responsible to the community, engages in activities related to the community's interests. Its activities are confined to the community members. These administrators aid in preserving calm in the school district's ethnic communities.

Those who are located at the central office may conduct in-service workshops and training for teachers, and other school personnel. Mostly though, they are engaged in administering and managing programs. They coordinate curricula, construct schedules, prepare reports, proposals and many other written materials. Those in the lower ranks are confined to their desks at the central office and they work primarily with each other or with minority teachers and principals. Those in higher ranks, such as the director, work with the superintendent, his associates and the school board. His responsibility is to explain the special projects, to see that the guidelines, rules and regulations are adhered to, and to inform the school district about the progress of the special projects.

Opportunity

Positions allocated to minorities are of various sorts. The most important characteristic is that with the exception of the top, usually the directorship position, all other positions do not lead to careers outside the special projects structure. They may lead to higher hierarchical posts within the same structure, but because they are defined as temporary, they are not likely to lead anywhere else.

There are, however, some opportunities afforded to minorities who would be denied any administrative experience in any other setting. First, these positions do permit the person to depart from teaching. Second, the post increases interaction with adults. Third, it affords increased visibility among minorities throughout the district. Fourth, as long as funds are available for these special projects, these persons are employed in posts which are better when compared to other minority possibilities.

The greatest opportunity is available to the highest post, the director. Because this office and the entire structure of special projects is dependent on external funds, there is a certain independence from the parent organization. Those directors who can continue to generate and increase funds can gradually assume considerable influence within the district. They can see to it that those employed within the structure benefit in specific ways to create loyalty and a following for them as well as for the structure. For example, travel funds can be made available to school personnel. Extra services, such as clerical and support services can be provided as well as specially equipped offices and classrooms. All of these aspects can create a structure which differs from the parent organization.

There is an additional component to this. Since the special projects are designed to align with community interests, the community can also provide a strong political force for it. This is, of course, due to its external support which increases its independence from the parent organization and maximizes structural autonomy.

Power

From the previous passage it can be seen how power can accrue to the directorship position if certain conditions are met. This power insures that minorities participate in the organization, that they occupy offices within the organization and that the moneys which are directed to them are spent among them.

This does not, however, insure that minorities are integrated within the organization. In fact, it may have an opposite effect in that the separate groups are strengthened and rigidified. Also, the power that is exerted by minorities is external over their own group. That aspect can create unrest among those who resent better conditions for minorities, but it does not disrupt the existing ties among them. Moreover, since decision-making posts are occupied by others, minorities are effectively immobile. These are severe limitations to the power available to minorities through the occupation of special projects administration.

PASSAGE THROUGH THE FUNCTIONAL BOUNDARY

It has been seen how minorities participate in a limited way within the school organization. The justification which has been provided is that embodied in the following passage from Contreras (1979). He writes:

> A great deal of time and energy (has been spent) in the recruitment of Spanish-surnamed administrators and other personnel. This is partly as a consequence of community pressure, on the assumption that these new personnel would a) be organizational members and provide role models for their ethnic group (models); b) provide recommendations for solutions to educational problems related to Hispanic community groups (expert); c) provide for communication with Hispanic community groups (link); or d) articulate and promote the needs and concerns of Hispanic community groups (advocate) (33).

As members of special projects they are able to fulfill the above expectations, at least to a limited degree.

This, however, does not explain the exclusion of minorities from the regular administrative positions: principal, central office post, and/or superintendent. Inkles (1973) states, "The critical test of the success of the socialization process lies in the ability of the individual to perform well in the statuses - that is, to play the roles - in which he may later find himself" (616).

Inkles (1973) presents four main elements in the socialization matrix:

> The main socialization issue, that is, the typical life condition or social demand which dominates the attention of the socializee and socializers, the agents of socialization, those individuals and social units or organizations which typically play the greatest role in the socialization process; the objectives which these agents set as the goals for successful socialization in each period, that is, the qualities they wish to inculcate and the conditions under which they prefer to train the socializee; and the main task facing the socializee, that is, the problem to be solved or the skill

learned as it confronts the socializee from his internal personal perspective (618).

Applying these four elements to minorities, several points can be raised. First, minorities placed in special projects do not face the issue, the school organization, in the same manner that the others do. But even if they are placed in a regular administrative post, they face an organization in which they are greatly outnumbered and in which they are perceived as different. This results in a condition which, from the start, differs from the conditions faced by others.

The second aspect is that the placement of minorities in special projects means that their socializing agents are minorities. If placed in regular administrative posts the socializing agents are likely to be members of the majority group. In either case, this difference in socializing agents means that minorities will not be socialized as others, because the majority are being socialized by the majority, while the minority are socialized by the majority.

The third consideration is the objectives. If it is accepted that minorities are to be socialized within their community and are to serve as models, experts, links, and advocates for the community and the school organization, it can be seen that it is efficient and rational to place minorities in special projects administration. In this way, minorities continue to interact with their community, persons from their community can thus use them as models and experts, and the school organization can use them as liaisons and advocates for both parties. But as was seen by the position of the area administrator's temporariness and the practice to limit the participation, an inoperative linkage function between the community and the organization existed. Moreover, the organizational objectives related to career mobility and success are not addressed for minorities. For those minority persons who wish to participate in the educational institution as others, their socialization is deficient if they are contained within special projects.

The fourth condition is the task facing the socializee. The task facing school administrators is school administration. Those groups or persons who are denied access to school administration and management tasks will not be socialized properly. Being confined to the special projects task, not only retains minorities there, but their movement elsewhere in the organization is also constrained.

The socialization process for minorities breaks down in the preparation for the principalship. As was shown in previous chapters the first administrative post in the school organization is the principalship. Failure to obtain that office denies a candidate an administrative career.

Valverde (1974) in his study of succession socialization to the principalship found certain factors which determined how minorities are excluded from the position. He defined succession socialization as being "only concerned with a candidate whose movement within an organization is a promotion and with the necessary learning he is subject to prior to formal acceptance" (4).

As was described earlier, minority teachers are placed in situations where their interaction and activities are limited to minority students. If as Valverde (1974) writes, "Succession socialization provides for promotion based on the preparation of candidates in a replicated fashion to perform administrative duties" (4) minorities must be placed where this replication is possible. Being confined to minority students, minority candidates do not have the opportunity to prepare in any fashion, much less in a replicated one, for an administrative post.

Additionally, it is at this time when a candidate learns the value system, the norms, and the required behavior patterns operant among the school administrators. This process is the result of two forces, the socializing agent and the socializing agency. The socializing agency is the school organization. Its agents are administrators. For a specific aspiring teacher, the agent would be the school site's principal. The two main ways in which the candidates are molded are by its working environment and the job activities (Valverde, 1974:9-10). Minorities being confined to activities related to minorities and being set apart from the rest are not provided with the socializing forces afforded to others.

The placement of individuals in the proper contexts to perform the attendant activities is important in socializing them. Becker (1964) describes this in the following passage. He writes:

The person as he moves in and out of a variety of social situations learns the requirements of continuing in each situation and of success in it. If he has a strong desire to continue, the ability to assess accurately what is required, and can deliver the required performance, the individual turns himself into the kind of person the situation demands (44).

The person who aids in this process is the sponsor. Valverde (1974) writes, "The sponsor performs a number of services for the protege which are manifested in various forms but which can be indexed into four categories. They are sanction, advice, protection, and exposure. All four of the categorical functions lead to promotion of the protege, the ultimate goal of sponsorship" (45).

Sanction is provided in the form of ratification for the candidate through the district's formal procedures, usually in the form of written ratings and references called for by the district's examination process (45).

Advice is directed to make the protege acceptable to significant others. The assumption is that if a candidate can gain the approval of his peers, then, he has the capability of gaining the approval of administrators. The objective is to shape the aspirant's behavior to be pleasing, agreeable and conforming, resulting in a codified behavior that mirrors the administrative reference group he/she is attempting to enter (64). Advice is also directed to shape a protege's administrative perspective to resemble the sponsor's (70). The concern for proteges is focused on who would view the protege displaying his/her talents (61).

Protection is mostly preventive or more specifically, not allowing the candidate to do or say anything that may harm his/her chance of advancing into administration. This protection is centered around not antagonizing any superiors. It is vital that the sponsor protect the protege from turning significant others from his favor (47).

The fourth category is to gain exposure. One way is through contact with other administrators (40). The training experiences provided by the sponsor are mainly for visibility and while the protege is undergoing these opportunities he is also being counseled. In brief, the type of activities assigned to the aspirant are assessed by the amount of exposure offered (60).

According to Valverde (1974) succession socialization occurs in several stages. The first is identification by sponsors. This is followed by the candidate expressing desire to be in administration and by undertaking additional extra-curricular activities beyond the normal classroom duties (52).

All of this is done in a subtle manner to be acceptable to others. As indicated by Blood (1966) one issue for those who departed from teaching to assume an administrative post was the degree of alienation. Those candidates most attached to teaching and other teachers experienced greater stress in departing from their group than did others. This is equally true for minorities. But more so, the stress is greater in being accepted into administration by others.

Adoption follows for those who gain acceptance among other administrators. This is the stage at which the candidate receives advice, training and additional experience. The last stage is the actual inculcation of values, behavioral patterns, attitudes and administration perspectives similar to those of the sponsor. Valverde refers to this as a replication process. In socialization terms it means that the candidate has changed from a non-administrator to an administrator.

Valverde (1974) charges that minorities are excluded from administration because they aren't sponsored. The problem seems to be more fundamental than that. While minorities are placed in minority settings and restrained to special projects, they will be unable to receive the opportunities which are necessary to gain access to administration. Therefore, the proper socialization processes for aspiring administrators begins during the period of teaching. Principals provide counsel and experience for candidates to progress.

In conclusion, because the acquisition of the first administrative post is dependent on sponsorship, minorities are shortchanged. But prior to that, the placement of minorities in favorable teaching positions will provide them with opportunities to display their abilities and capabilities so that sponsorship may be more readily accessible.

The literature does not record the process by which minorities advance beyond the principalship. One reason is that there are very few minorities holding line central office positions and the superintendency. Since in this study, the sample of minorities included line position holders several observations can be reported. First, minorities are likely to move more frequently, but not necessarily upwardly. For example, out of a total of 107 minority persons, 43 held line positions; the principalship, associate superintendency and superintendency. There were also 16 directors and two area administrators included in the sample. The rest were positions such as coordinator, resource teacher, and others. (See Table 12.)

Most of the persons in the sample had recently obtained their posts. The few exceptions included the three Mexican-American superintendents and three principals: one Black and two Mexican-Americans. The directorships were all dependent on external funds and all of these positions were held for less than two years. Because this section is concerned with the principalship, line central office positions, and the superintendent the discussion will deal with them.

THE PRINCIPALSHIPS

As was stated earlier, the two primary ways of obtaining the principalship was in the traditional promotional manner and in this sample those who were administrators prior to the mid-sixties had obtained their posts in this way. This included two Mexican-American and one Black principal. They were placed in schools where their particular ethnic group was predominant and referred to as "conservative before the movement" types. It was also generally acknowledged that they had obtained their positions because they were highly trained and had earned them. They had been in their school districts a long time or came strongly supported from surrounding districts.

The greater number of principalships were obtained during the late sixties and early seventies. The position holders were younger than their white colleagues, had less school experience, and in some cases were appointed without any administrative preparation. They were appointed from the teaching ranks because a school was in trouble. Usually, this appointment came after the school year had started.

Hierarchy

As was stated earlier, when minorities are placed in minority schools, their hierarchical position is below that of the rest of the principals. This is as a consequence of several factors. First, minority schools are viewed as different from the rest. Second, the placement of an individual in a minority school is a signal to the rest of the school district that there is a difference between them. Third, the placement of an individual in a minority school is not viewed by the rest of the organization as a reward. Also, others in the organization do not actively seek to be placed in a minority school. Therefore, serving as a minority principal in a minority school means being hierarchically below other principals but above teachers.

Organizational Space
Working Environment

Minority principals' schools contain "hard-to-teach" students, beginning teachers, and/or teachers who have been unable to move to "better" schools, and other minority teachers, and poorly maintained buildings. These principals are expected to "contain" the student unrest and community complaints, but are not readily allowed to make changes regarding the physical plant, personnel or curriculum.   Therefore, minority principals work in inaccessible, unpleasant school sites with other minorities.

Interpersonal Relationships

Because of the initial placement of minority principals, they are seldom known by the rest of the school personnel. The nature of their appointment contributes to skepticism about their capabilities. Without a sponsor, each minority remains alone. The result is that even though these persons have departed from teaching, they have not departed from the attendant characteristics of minorities.

Their interaction is confined to those in their schools and their attendance area.   It is problematic for minority principals to develop both extensive and intensive interpersonal relationships outside of their ethnic group.

Nevertheless, there are important changes between the principalship and teaching.   The person is now interacting with adults and must at least to a limited degree, interact with other principals and central office staff.   In this sense, there are opportunities to develop extensive interpersonal relationships.

Activities

Minority principals are granted their position to calm the campus (student unrest) and to contain the community.   They are not expected to bother the teaching staff or other school personnel. Others within the school district do not expect them to be administrators nor managers.   Moreover, occupation of the principalship by minorities is viewed as a temporary condition. This leads to minority principals' preoccupation with students.

Granted, that minority principals' concerns continue to be centered on students, holding the post, nevertheless does provide opportunities for administering and managing a school site which differs in marked ways from a classroom.   Thus, the principal has new and expanded activities which distinguish administration from teaching.

Opportunity

The principalship for minorities is an advancement in comparison to other minorities. It is not in comparison to others. Because of the different expectations for minorities, advancement to other positions is problematic. Nonetheless, even for minorities, this post does contain opportunities for movement elsewhere.

PASSAGE THROUGH THE INCLUSION BOUNDARY
Permeability

Since minorities occupy the principalship without sponsorship, certain dysfunctions occur. First, if the placement of the minority person is prior to the acquisition of an administrative credential, the person occupies the position without acceptance by other administrators. Second, the precise expectation being to solve a social problem in the school rather than to administer or manage, serves to restrain the individual. Third, the absence of a sponsor means that the minority person does not have a support system or someone to call on for help. These factors serve to separate the minority principal from the rest of the principals.

This separation takes several forms both formally and informally. One means is not to invite minority principals to administrative meetings. For example, several principals stated something to this effect, "The first indication I got that I wasn't going to be treated like the rest of the administrators was that they had meetings and I wasn't notified. When I inquired I was told that the meeting wasn't concerned with minority children or topics" (March, 1978).

All principals are invited to the principals' meetings, but even in this, differences are noted. Minority principals don't actively participate. They are singled out to become minority experts. For example, a Black principal was appointed to a committee to plan the district's means for commemorating Martin Luther King's Day. A Hispanic principal was responsible for coordinating the bilingual activities among several schools.

Another indication of this separation is in the appointments to special district-wide committees requiring ethnic expertise but their almost total absence in all other committees. Some explained this was so because many demands were placed upon minority administrators. Some also implied that minority persons just weren't as interested in district-wide affairs as others.

Informally, minorities are likewise excluded from participation. In the present study, none of the minority principals were part of the regular informal groups.

As stated earlier, when minority principals are appointed, it is not expected they will remain in that post for long. Therefore, those relationships, duties, and activities in which they engage are not fostered by other administrators. The result is that minority principals are not aided in the socialization process. They are not expected to change and they are not expected to be successful administrators. There are, however, a few minority principals who are successful in spite of the barriers which exist. They do become successful administrators and do manage to retain their posts. There are even a few who manage to advance.

Filtering Properties

Keeping in mind that minority principals in many cases obtained their positions because the school was in trouble, these persons may not seem as indispensable after the difficulty has been settled. In this case, these principals may be pressured to "move on." This is particularly apt to happen if the person did not have an administrative credential at the time the position was assumed. But, it can also happen because as the school gets settled, personnel may complain, or the school may appear more favorable to others.

The person who presses for permanency in these principalship positions finds that the system balks by several means. There is an increase in work load, an increase of variety within the work load; the schedule is changed to increase inconveniences, the individual may be placed under very crowded conditions; a reorganization takes place, and finally a negative evaluation is submitted to the central office.

Minorities comply in one of three ways: 1) they quit or move, 2) they successfully comply; 3) they decide to comply in some ways but not in others. Confrontation follows in both of the latter cases. The organization readily accepts the first option. The second option is usually taken by women. This is viewed as inconceivable by the central office superiors. Women who fulfill this expectation are described as "super gals, wonder women, fools, queen bees, and strange ones without friends." Minority males are more likely to select the third option.

Those who select to comply in some ways but not in others pretend they "can handle it." They do this in several forms. They never catch up with their work. They refuse to come early or stay late. Their "visiting increases if they're isolated or placed in crowded conditions," and they "create the most unpleasant situation when they receive a negative evaluation," said an associate superintendent (April, 1977). One minority male described what happened when he was told he was being sent back to the classroom. "I got up, doubled my fist, I swore up and down and scared the ____ out of the associate superintendent. I told him in no uncertain terms that he'd better prepare the rest of his superiors for my coming" (March, 1977). This person is still principal.

Another example is that of a minority woman principal who expected to remain in that position indefinitely as a Hispanic junior high school principal. She was told that her contract wasn't being renewed. The main reason was that in the process of straightening out the school she had made many teachers and others unhappy. She expressed it this way, "What did they expect? That I come in and clean up what was their accumulated garbage and not make enemies? Of course, I made enemies. I straightened out the school in two years. Now, I'm accused of being a difficult person" (July, 1978).

The associate superintendent for personnel said of the same person, "Actually, she did very well! We expected her to end up in a psychiatric ward or medical center. She did improve the school, but you see that's not normal. People of her race can't do things like that! People here just don't like or understand her" (September, 1978). She had to leave the school district.

From these examples, it can be seen that minorities, even though occupying the principalship position, may be halted in their careers due to the types of expectations held for them.

Out of the 107 minority persons in this sample, 43 were principals. Of these, two Hispanic female mid-high school principals, one Hispanic male high school principal, one mid-high and one high school Black female principals, and one high school Black male principal became assistant superintendents. All of these changes were to another school district. One Hispanic high school principal became a director of special projects within the same school district. Among the Black women principals, one mid-high principal became a special projects director. All other principals remained as principals, or were sent back to the classroom, or placed in special projects.

Those minority principals who are successful develop a very distinctive role. First, they reveal a sensitivity and an understanding about the problems of minorities without dwelling on hopelessness. Second, they have a repertoire of behaviors which are operant in the company of their ethnic groups as well as with other school personnel. There is a sense of appropriateness which they bring to each separate setting or group. For example, Contreras (1979) reports that in his study the Spanish-surnamed educational administrators faced situations of potential conflict involving simultaneous but opposing expectations of the educational institution and Hispanic community groups as administrators rather than as ethnic representatives and did not experience deep community rejection because of it. At the same time, they often responded as ethnic advocates and did not, as a consequence, experience deep institutional rejection because of it (39).

Third, these persons are highly independent and strong willed so that those who wish to denigrate them are unable to affect them; and when problems arise, they are able to confront them without requiring "propping from superiors." These individuals are highly aware of the personal consequences for their shortcomings. They know they will lose their jobs readily if they falter. The result is that these persons do not overreact, do not unnecessarily alarm anyone and do not procrastinate when something needs to be done.

In other words, the socialization process which minorities undergo in trying to be successful administrators enables them to develop a strong sense of mission and accomplishment. A characteristic that becomes evident is an intensity about their work which is absent in those who progress in a more leisurely fashion.

In considering the implications for socialization among minorities, it can be seen that those who are successful administrators have changed in two fundamental ways: 1) they have adapted to the organizational demands to the highest degree, partly to continuously prove their worth, but primarily in order to hold on to their positions and advance; 2) they have come to terms with their ethnicity and what it means in their lives. Those who are extremely adept can move from one context to another with ease. Those less adept are most likely to be suspect in both contexts. In that case, these persons adjust to marginal status in both settings, but their primary interest is occupational. Success in administration means that ethnicity is secondary, but ever present.

As has been seen, minorities are seldom sponsored into positions and are seldom supported by superiors. The overall result is that most minorities' top position is the principalship. However, for those who wish to advance beyond the principalship sponsorship of some sort is imperative.

CENTRAL OFFICE

As was said earlier, central office positions are granted as rewards for accomplishments in school sites or projects. Minorities may gain access to the central office in one of two ways. If the person has been successful in generating and increasing funds and proven to possess agreeable interpersonal skills as director of special projects, he may be advanced to assistant superintendent. During the period of this study, out of sixteen directors, three became assistant superintendents. These are persons who are personable, well known in the school district and have developed a community following.

The more common way to obtain an associate, assistant, deputy superintendency is to have had experience in the secondary schools. While there, the superintendent may be impressed with the improvements at the secondary school and the person may be invited into the central office. Minorities are likely to move from a secondary principalship in one school district to a central office post in another. This is so because the most likely sponsor is the superintendent and the "safest" referral system is to another superintendent who brings the minority person in as an outsider.

This raised the important issue about minorities and their advancement pattern. Whereas internal advancement for others is common in school districts, for minorities it is not. One reason is the tenuous sponsorship system to which they're attached. As one superintendent said:

> I know Rafael can be successful. He's one of the brightest persons I've ever known, but this school district is suspicious of Hispanics. I would be pressured to consider

another person. Rafael could be pressured to do more and better and it just wouldn't work as well. So, what I've done is refer him to Sun City School District. I know the superintendent there. He's been impressed with Rafael. Rafael will be a newcomer and pressures will be more in line with those of a newcomer, rather than those related to his ethnicity (February, 1978).

Minorities are also aware of this problem and one assistant superintendent described his move in this way, "I would have problems with my credibilitiy in the other district. They know me as a Black activist. They're still a little suspicious. In this district, I have a lot to learn and people will gradually learn to work with me and accept me" (March 1978).

As central office line administrators, minorities continue to change in accordance to the organizational demands. Their personal attitudes adjust in order to give primacy to the organization. Even as they continue to view themselves as separate from others, their perception of what organizational success entails sharpens. For example, one of the minority assistant superintendents who'd just been a secondary principal states:

> As soon as I learned to view myself as others do in this context, I was able to make decisons regarding my work in an entirely different way. I know most of my colleages do not think I'm equal to them. In that case, their treatment of me will be different. I must deal with that. I know what I can do. I know I can do it better than most. My job is to prove it publicly. As long as I keep that in mind, I can continue to advance. Not without pain, but I won't be stopped (December 1976).

By the time minorities obtain central office positions, several pronounced differences between the groups are evident. This is a result of differences in their socialization processes. For example, as minorities participate with others, they are reticent to share experiences. There are two reasons for this. First, their experiences are likely to deal with their ethnic group since they tend to head schools with heavy ethnic enrollments. Recounting experiences would just exacerbate the stereotyping that is already prevalent. Second, one of the functions of sharing experiences or recounting "war stories" is to learn from others. In the case of minorities, other administrators aren't particularly interested in "those schools." They don't view minorities' experiences as relevant to their work. Therefore, minorities do not discuss their work experiences with others.

Rather, minority males participate in a very different way. They serve as integraters, synthesizers, and ice-breakers. They do this by applying witticism, wise sayings, proverbs, jokes and one-liners to the regular conversations being carried on by the school administrators. For example, one director collected quotations which he kept augmenting in a binder.   This practice permits minority males to participate easily in a group.   It serves to relax other male administrators and it detracts from the seriousness of interacting with a minority.   Successful minority administrators reflect a gregarious, cheerful, charming, and easy-going personality. Some examples of one-liners are:

"Every successful person has to contend with approval."
"We are all born free but raised in captivity."
"Use the rear view mirror only for reference."
"Big shots are little shots who keep on shooting."
"Small men talk about things; average men talk about people; great men talk about ideas."
"Bite the bullet, sort of speak."
"Never look back unless you intend to go that way."

Minority women behave more like white women than minority males.   They are excluded from informal conversational exchange, they don't joke and in general maintain a very proper low profile.

HISPANIC FEMALE ADMINISTRATORS

Because this researcher was particularly interested in determining the participation of Hispanic female administrators, 55 were selected for further study.   Out of these, 16 were elementary principals, 3 mid-high principals, 2 specialists, 20 special projects coordinators, 10 special projects specialists and 4 special projects supervisors.

As can be seen from this breakdown, most of the Hispanic women are located in special projects administration.   The greater number of those remaining are elementary principals.   Out of the three mid-high principals, two became assistant superintendents during the course of the study.

Out of the 55 administrators, 10 had been hired as school teachers before the mid-sixties.   All others were hired during the mid-sixties and afterwards.   Therefore, this group is comparatively young, particularly with regard to white women adminstrators. Whereas, Gross and Trask (1976) report four-fifths of their sample of women being fifty years of age or older, and Drust's (1976) study showed that the California woman administrator's average age was 52, 50% of the Chicano administrators were under 39 years of age and 85% were under 50 years of age (Ortiz and Venegas, 1978).

Those women who had been hired prior to the mid-sixties were holding teaching and elementary principalships at that time.   During the conflict of the mid-sixties one elementary principal became a mid-high principal.   The other two mid-high principals came directly from the classroom.   In all of these cases, the women were hired to "straighten out the school."

Other posts which were available to those teaching prior to the mid-sixties were in special projects.   Some of them became supervisors and coordinators. Two elementary principals remained as elementary principals, but were transferred from school to school within the school district as their need for "straightening out" the schools arose. One of these principals held a post in three different schools during the course of the study.

Since most of the Hispanic female school administrators were hired during the mid-sixties and afterwards, they were inclined to have entered their school district by other means, besides the regular teacher credentialed way. Some entered without a teaching credential, obtained it during their stay and ultimately also obtained their administrative credential.

Those Hispanic female administrators in special projects have experienced different stresses from those holding the regular administrative positions. Since these woman have not departed from children nor instruction nor their ethnic group, their perspectives about education and their place within the school organization have not had to be greatly modified. Rather, the difficulties they encounter in their work are related to providing better educational and instructional services to students. In conjuction with this concern they are also aware of their peculiar status within the school district. They realize they are not part of the regular school faculties' social systems. They also realize that they may not be receiving their due share as participating members of the the organization. In general, these problems are resolved by concentrating on minority students' concerns. They do this by allocating time, energy and resources to their students.

In contrast, Hispanic female principals find themselves heading institutions which are in serious trouble. Moreover, these principals are assigned to these schools to improve conditions which range from physical deterioration to student apathy and/or destructiveness. Not to be discounted, is the fact that the existing teaching personnel is predominately non-Hispanic, unhappy and on occasion alienated.

As an example of the type of "administration and management" responsibility which these women face, a description of one of the two elementary principals' posts will be provided.

The two Hispanic female elementary principals who were observed were individuals who had obtained their education in the local prestigious universities. One of them was completing her doctorate from a nearby private institution and both had taught ten years before obtaining their first administrative position and had prior administrative experience serving as vice principals and teaching principals. Both had also strong support from their superiors. Their administrative experience as principals during their first two years, prior to the mid-sixties was comparable to other principals with the exception that they taught and administered minority schools. Nonetheless, their recollection are that the expectations for their work and roles changed during the mid-sixties.

During the mid-sixties both administrtators headed comparatively good minority schools. In fact, their schools were used as models of what minority schools were capable of being. When conflict arose in the surrounding schools, both principals were transferred during the latter part of the year to other schools. One of them recounts:

> I was called in to the central office. I was told about this school which had just been severely damaged and vandalized. Finally, I was told I was assigned to it. That afternoon, the associate superintendent and a board member and I toured the plant. The following morning I faced a group of parents, school board members, and the top school officials in a session in which I was told precisely what I was expected to accomplish in that school. That afternoon I moved to the other school. As soon as I stepped onto those grounds I went to work. For three months I met, talked, figured, argued, compromised, listened, and labored. The school was cleaned up, the students calmed down and the teachers seemed to be happier (September 1976).

During the summer months, the principal had the school painted, the grounds improved, and ordered new instructional materials. When school began in the fall, the school appeared very much like the school she had left half a year before.

A couple of months went by and she was called to the central office again. A repeat of the previous year followed. The principal was placed in a different school. The expectations were the same. The accomplishments were fulfilled and she stayed in that school for two years.

At the time of the study she had just been assigned to another school. She was in the midst of "straightening it out" but she expressed tiredness of this "sort of life." She brought about improvements to the school and remained there for two years. She was later reassigned to another school with similar problems. Again, she improved the school but decided she was tired of moving from school to school. When she was asked to move to another school two years later, she refused. She stayed another year, but during this period, parents and teachers united to submit charges to the superintendent and school board against her. At the end of the data collection period, the principal was in the process of moving to another school.

The description presented above is used as an illustration of the type of career Hispanic female principals may establish. All Hispanic female principals were held to similar expectations and all were subjected to similar experiences, albeit, with not as many and as rapid changes. Nevertheless, the organizational perspective about their role is clear. These women are viewed as "warriors" who bring about stability in minority schools.

There is another aspect to this practice. Since these women represent a particular ethnic group which willingly or unwillingly is misunderstood, school officials are likely to relinquish all responsibilities for the school to the minority person. For example, an elementary female principal said:

I wanted to host a back-to-school night in the fall. I invited the superintendent and school board members. The superintendent said, "Look, it's your school, they're your people. You speak their language, you know their ways. You can have the whole affair! I'd attend, but I think I might intrude. It's better if you do everything by yourself." None of the school officials showed up (April 1975).

Another example of the manner in which school officials relinquish responsibilities for the school is when a principal needed some playground equipment and textbooks.

The associate superintendent said, "But those children don't read or know how to play with that equipment. Besides, if you really want to dare to teach them, ask the Title I and Title VII directors to find some funds for you" (March 1976).

A mid-high principal stated that once when her school was hosting a dance, she called to have the central office personnel come over. None of them could work it in their schedules to visit.
Another mid-high principal had her students perform outstandingly in some swimming, track and gymnastic meets. She asked that some recognition be given from the central office. None was granted. Later in the year, the band and chorus were awarded recognition for their work. No one from the central office acknowledged it.
These principals feel that they and their schools are not perceived as others. Their belief is that the school officials' concerns are to contain the schools. A deputy superintendent stated:

When those schools do something outstanding it is just a fluke. You can't depend on those communities or those students. Moreover, the principal has just been lucky. She has a good school now because there aren't any problems (March 1976).

Hispanic female principals are tokens in the general structure of school administrtation. They are treated as such and they are expected to portray either the sultry Latin character or the Virgen de Guadalupe image. In both cases, these expectations require a repertoire of behaviors which don't alarm others because of their stereotyped preconceptions, but at the same time display skills and competencies in school administration. The women who are successful are extremely wary and highly possessive of their positions. They view themselves realistically in comparision to the rest of the school organization. They remain ever ready to defend themselves and fight for their positions. In addition, they develop loyalty and tenacity towards their work and the organization. They learn to assess what is possible and to pace themselves to accomplish whatever is necessary. One mid-high principal on her acquisition of the assistant superintendency of personnel position stated:

> Well, I've obtained this post. It has required time and energy. Now, I must prepare for the next battle, and the next. You see, now I must keep this post for a reasonable period of time. I don't doubt a war will result. I must be ready. If I expect to advance, I must continue in this way. There's no alternative (February 1979).

The other group of Hispanic female administrators is made up of very young, inexperienced persons. As they assume their positions as elementary principals, their roles are prescribed more definitely than for others. First, their assignments are to minority schools. These assignments are granted with the hope that they can contain their schools. As is true with minority males, they are not expected to retain their positions for long nor are they expected to become administrators and managers. Second, these individuals are assigned by community groups, the school board, and the superintendent in concert. There is no person or group of persons who can be identified as a supporting system. One of their most traumatic experiences is to realize that they can call on no one to help them if they run into a problem. One newly appointed elementary principal related:

> I had been at my job for two weeks. I received this memo from the central office to submit a physical plant inventory. I looked all over for a physical plant inventory. I could not find one. I realized I had accepted the post without asking for one; I now had to produce one. I called another principal whom I thought would understand my problem. He just laughed and said, "Good luck." I called on the other minority principals. They either said they didn't know what I was talking about or they just laughed. Finally, I called the central office. They just said, "Well, if you can't find a copy of a previous inventory, you'll have to conduct one now and provide it for us." I later found out that that school had not had an inventory submitted since 1965 (January 1979).

Third, because these women are on their own, there is no one after whom they can model their behavior. Senior male adminstrators either totally ignore them so that no one ever knows the extent of their abilities and capacities or else they are severely taunted and teased. The point is that these persons do not have the opportunities to learn to be administrators under the conditions that others do. For this reason, they are the most likely candidates to be unable to retain their administrative positions and thereby advance at the same rate as others.

Therefore, Hispanic female administrators change in three fundamental ways. First, they must change their perspectives about the cultural role of women. Second, they must change their views about the organization as they progress from children and instruction to adults and administration concerns. Third, they must change regarding the way they obtain and hold their administrative positions. Skills, knowledge, and experience are not adequate. They must develop a possessiveness and loyalty to their work which will support them as they battle for retention of their administrative positions.

THE SUPERINTENDENT

This position eludes most minorities. In this case, only one person was promoted to the superintendency during the period of the study. The other three superintendents were already in that post. Of these three only one remains as the superintendent of the same school district. One of the other two changed superintendencies to a different district and within two years left to accept a state appointment. The other superintendent left the superintendency of his school district during the last year of this study to accept a federal post in Washington, D.C.. All of these superintendents have doctorates from prestigious universities. With the exception of the principal who became superintendent during the study, all have headed school districts of 20,000 or more enrollment.

These persons have reconciled the organizational demands with their personal needs. One of the minority superintendents said:

It took me a long time to realize I am in this alone. I am responsible for keeping my job and there are many who want it. I also learned that every time I admit some weakness, someone will use it to downgrade me. I spend a great deal of time seeing to it that I remain strong, that the school district does those things which reflect its strength and that everyone is systematically reminded about this. The main reason I have to think this way is because whereas other administrators are expected to be successful, I am not. My burden to to prove that I am not a failure (September 1977).

CONCLUSION

There are very few minorities in educational administration. Additionally, those few are concentrated in schools and school districts where their ethnic group is dominant. There are several reasons why this pattern persists.

First, minorities are placed in minority schools to provide role models for their group. Second, minorities are expected to teach those areas which are connected to their ethnic group. Third, in order to maintain a linkage between the ethnic group and the school, a sub-structure is created for minorities. This structure is institutionalized as special projects. Within this, minorities are advanced from teaching to various supervisory and administrative positions. The top office in this unit is the directorship. Aside from this post, all other offices are limited in opportunites and the accumulation of power. The directorship provides a rare opportunity for movement to an assistant superintendency.

Minority principals are placed in minority schools. As heads of these schools they are perceived and treated differently from other principals and school administrators. The predispositions to limit minority adminstrators to minority schools leads to a continuing separation between them.

Beyond contributing to separate groups of administrators, minorities are also denied the same socialization process others undergo. This difference subsequently leads to minority males participating in a limited fashion. On a formal basis, they provide the expertise regarding minority issues. On an informal basis, they provide witticisms, one-liners and quotatations as they integrate, summarize and synthesize conversations, shared experiences and "war stories" presented by the white male leaders.

NOTES

[1]Data reported is from the EEO-5 survey which is conducted annually by mail questionnaire for a stratified random sample of school districts with 250 or more students. Employment in such districts corresponds to the employment size cut-off for Title VII coverage.

In selecting the sample, all school districts were stratified by enrollment size and location. All school districts in the central city of a Standard Metropolitan Statistical Area (SMSA), as well as those districts with 1,800 or more students were included in the survey. A systematic random sample was taken of the remaining school districts in accordance with enrollment size and the desired percent coverage shown below:

Stratum	Enrollment	Full-time Employment	Percent Sampled
1	1,800	100	100
2	900–1799	50–99	50
3	500–899	25–49	25
4	250–499	15–24	15
5	1–249	1–14	0

[2]Mexican-Americans are usually considered as part of the Hispanic population. This group is concentrated in the five

southwestern states: California, Texas, Arizona, Colorado, and New Mexico. Statistics regarding this group are also more readily available than for other Hispanic ones.

[3]Information gathered in the "U.S. Commission of Civil Rights Spring 1969 Mail Survey of Mexican-American Education in the Southwest" and the Commission's tabulations of "The Fall 1968 Elementary and Secondary School Survey" conducted by the U.S. Department of Health, Education and Welfare (HEW) under Title VI of the Civil Rights Act of 1964.

CHAPTER 6

Application to Socialization And Role Theories

Educational administration has been analyzed in several different ways. First, it has been seen how three groups in educational administration acquire various roles which ultimately result in differing socialization processes and careers for them. White males assume the roles of teacher, vice-principal, principal, central office administrator, and finally the superintendency. Women, on the other hand, tend to pursue two types of careers. On one, they assume the roles of teacher and elementary principal. On the other, they become specialists, supervisors, and on rare occasions assistant superintendents of instruction. Minorities, also, begin by assuming the role of teacher. In contrast to the other two groups, they are more likely to advance in school administration as special projects administrators.

Second, it can be seen that the structure of educational administration consists of white males occupying line positions, women occupying staff positions, and minorities occupying special projects. Third, the structure shows that white males manage and administer adults, women instruct children, and minorities direct and contain other minorities. Figure 1 illustrates the comprehensive structure of educational administration.

As has been stated throughout this study the three groups which have been described undergo different socialization processes which ultimately lead to either success or failure to acquire the superintendency. What is demonstrated is that a certain sequence of positions which permit specific experiences are acquired which may or may not prepare an individual to obtain the superintendency position. It is the differing patterns in the occupation of certain positions and not others which determine the differing types of careers available to school administrators. This chapter will present those theoretical strands which have been developed that indicate situational factors which lead to predictable differences among persons pursuing certain careers. Both socialization and role theory developments will be outlined to show how social science does provide a means for anticipating certain consequences.

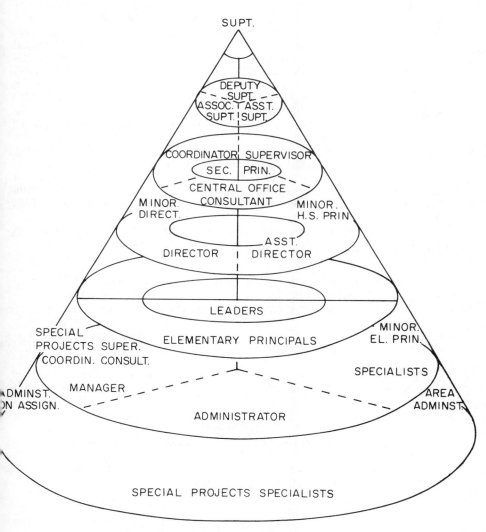

Figure 1. *Structure of Educational Administration*

SOCIALIZATION THEORY: HISTORICAL DEVELOPMENT
Sociological Views

From the beginning there has been an attempt to characterize socialization as a continuing process in which two common threads are presented. The "participation of the individual in collective activities" and the "idea that socialization includes the gradual incorporation by the individual of the beliefs and customs of his society or group" (Clausen, 1968:23). For example, Simmel in 1895 wrote that "socialization referred to the process of group formation or development of the forms of association" (22). Giddings (1897) later defined socialization as the "development of a social nature or character - social state of mind - in the individuals who associate" (2). A similar idea was expressed by Ross (1896) when he wrote "the molding of the individual's feelings and desires to suit the needs of the group...(is) the highest and most difficult work of society" to be accomplished partly through "social influence" and partly through "social control." He referred to this moulding as the "socialization of the members of the group" (In Clausen, 1968: 22-23).

Ernest Burgess presented similar views in The Function of Socialization in Social Revolution (1916). McDougall (1908) in the same vein wrote:

If we would understand the life of societies, we must first learn to understand the way in which individuals become moulded by the society in which they are born and in which they grow up, how by this moulding they become fitted to play their part in it as social beings and how, in short, they become capable of moral conduct" (174).

Another researcher, Dewey (1922), describing the "shaping" function of social interaction, wrote:

Connections with our fellows furnish both the opportunities for action and the instrumentalities by which we take advantage of opportunity...If the standard of morals is low, it is because the social environment is defective...If a child gets on by peevishness and intrigue, then, others are his accomplices who assist in the habits which are built up (317-319).

Charles Horton Cooley (1922), who was concerned with the ways in which human nature was shaped by participation in the social order, presented several themes in his writings. These themes covered: 1) the relationship of the individual to society; 2) early sociability of children; 3) role taking expressed as "by imagining what we would do in various situations," "drawing upon our experience with others," and "trying them in various situations"; 4) the crucial importance of the primary-group relationship for the development of personality and for a conception of human nature" (in Clausen, 1968:25-26); and 5) the mechanics of learning social roles by the constant process of evaluation by others and one's subsequent adjustment in behavior in accordance with such evaluation" (Boshoff, 1922:40; Cooley, 1902: 152).

Thomas (1896), expressing the same sentiment, wrote, "Problems of the synthesis of human personalities are not problems of personal status but problems of personal becoming" (In Polish Peasant, 1918-1920:1843).

It is seen, then, that in the 1920's, socialization was "predominately used to refer to the 'shaping' of the person and to the mechanisms whereby individuals were transformed into persons" (Clausen, 1968:24).

For example, Burgess' (1916) studies on the attitudes, standards, and philosophy of life of the criminal demonstrated the potency of this view. A case in point is Shaw's The Jack Roller (1930) which explains the delinquent career as a consequence of "social conditioning" in a milieu that oriented the individual toward illegitimate activities and provided him with skill-training in such activities rather than conventional pursuits.

It was not until 1939 that the term socialization came to be at all widely used in its present sense.   Park (1939) wrote of the "progressive socialization of the world, that is, the incorporation of all peoples of the earth in a worldwide economy, which had laid the foundation for the rising world-wide political and moral order" (Park, 1939:23).   Dollard (1939) at the same time argued for a "unification of scientific approaches... to study socialization " which he defined as "the process of training a human animal from birth on for social participation in his group" (Dollard, 1939:60). At the same time, two sociology textbooks, Ogburn and Nimhoff (1940) and Sutherland and Woodward (1937), were written on the "process whereby the individual is converted into the person," namely, "socialization" (in Clausen, 1968:25).

Socialization continued to be a topic of interest to those researchers who studied the impact of schools on students. Durkheim (1956), in Education and Sociology, characterized education as "the influences exercised by adult generations on those that are not ready for social life.   Its object is to arouse and to develop in the child a certain number of physical, intellectual and moral states which are demanded of him both by the political society as a whole and the special milieu for which he is specifically destined"(71).

In the same vein, Himmelweit and Sealy (1966), in the The School as an Agent of Socialization outline the impact of schooling on children in Great Britain.   Turner (1960) also dealt with the same subject in his contrast of the nature of selective and preparatory operations of the schools in the United States and England.   All of these researchers' efforts were directed at showing how schooling served to "shape" future citizens.

George Herbert Mead (1934) in the forefront dealt with the basic aspects of socialization — "to the rise of meaning and of selfhood in the process of social interaction" (Clausen, 1968:28). His contributions are his detailed analyses of the "establishment of communication and the process through which meanings arise in social interaction/ He gave special attention to the development of the self in the place of caretaker, for example, and become an 'object to himself'" (in Clausen, 1968:28).

As is seen from the review just presented, sociological contribution to socialization research has been most notable in the realm of adolescent and adult socialization. In this area socialization is, to a large extent, described as a matter of role learning. Such studies of socialization have frequently taken place in the context of a particular observation and the use of interviews or questionnaires.

Conceptual Development

The studies dealing with adjustment of an individual to a particular setting have employed several concepts. One of these has been normlessness. This concept has appeared as "anomie" (Durkheim, 1956; Merton, 1938). For example, Robert Merton has seen anomie as the ultimate product of a culture whose institutionalized means were inconsistent with its accepted goals – in clear reference to the American scene. His theoretical stance was presented in technical essays for professional sociologists and within the context of the 1930's when traditional ends and means appeared less sustaining than they have since become. The term "anomie" has not, however, played a major role in his later essays, even those addressed to his fellow sociologists. It has instead continued to enter into discussions as the socio-psychological level and into the assessment of such deviant behavioral patterns as delinquency, crime, suicide, and radicalism (Fredricks, 1970:57).

Conformity, on the other hand, has been the more honored concept. For example, David Reisman et al's The Lonely Crowd (1961) has become part of the growing body of literature in this area. In fact, conformity has been taken up by scores of researchers and developed extensively through the nineteen-fifties. The country's business elite and the larger public saw it elaboratred and popularized in the The Organization Man (1956).

Conformity was also studied in light of community life. These studies, whose prototypes appeared in the Lynd's Middletown volumes in the late twenties and thirties and Vidich and Bensman's (1960) Small Town in Mass Society are but some examples.

Related to these studies, other works such as Aldous Huxley's Brave New World, (1932) appeared which included not only the state of the victim but also the nature of the villain. Here the art of manipulation was given top billing. The more highly developed description of manipulation was portrayed in the Mills' (1956) The Power Elite as an interlaced and interchangeable network within the highest echelons of industry, government, and the military (In Clausen, 1968:60).

These studies depict the layman as the product of a manipulated conformity. The works displaying this view include Erich Fromm's (1941) Escape From Freedom and The Sane Society (1951).

In summary, what is shown in the works dealing with socialization is that forces are identified which act upon individuals to varying degrees. The evidence presented is persuasive and represents many perspectives. What is surprising is that this research has served to describe rather than as an instrument of social reform.

PSYCHOLOGICAL VIEWS

In psychology, socialization was not a major focus of attention until the 1930's. Even though socialization incorporates learning and the development of some theories of learning, most learning theorists have not had major interest in the larger process by which an individual is prepared for full partipation in adult life. The study of personality orientations and organization and the formulation of theories of personality has given impetus to socialization theory and research, but the linkages between the two have not been direct.

Psychologists have tended to look less closely at the origin of socialization emphases and more closely at the immediate relationship between agent and inductee. They have been especially concerned with establishing the nature of the processes mediating between socialization practices and child behavior, such as identification, the development of conscience, stages or dynamics of cognitive structuring, and the shape of motivational dispositions. As a consequence, they have conceptualized and studied child behavior itself to a far greater extent than have socialization researchers from other disciplines. Psychologists have, however, neglected the study of adult outcomes of socialization practices.

Among those researchers prior to the 30's, Baldwin (1913), realizing the influence of social aspects, wrote:

> Culture: a body of beliefs, usages and sanctions are transmitted entirely by social means, and administered to growing individuals by example, precept, and discipline...It constitutes the milieu, a body of influences which are necessary for the development of the individual mind. Such functions as language, spoken and written, play and art, such inventions as fire, building, and weaving, are not only conveniences of life; they are necessary means of growth (Baldwin, J., 1913a:129-130).

He referred to play and imitation as the "tools of 'socialization according to nature.'" He explained that the meanings of life situations are learned in play and imitation when the child "tries on the varied ways of doing things and so learns his own capacities and limitations" (Baldwin, 1911:20).

Allport (1924) employed the term socialization somewhat as we do today. He stated:

In order to be adapted to a civilized society, a man must not only be sensitive to the social objects about him; he must also develop permanent habits of response which are in accord with the necessities of group life.   Such development may be called the socialization of the indivdual.   It consists of a modification of the original and prepotent reflexes through instruction received in the social environment (Allport, 1924:123).

Clark Hull and John Dollard's (1935) primary focus was on adult personality.   Their work foreshadowed several themes which were to be important in the psychological work on socialization during the forties and fifties.   One of these was the use of laboratory experimental methods to study such processes (Clausen, 1968:36-38).

At Harvard under the leadership of Henry Murray, personality was studied as a "dynamic process, to be understood in terms of the reconstructed biography of the individual." Murray (1938) wrote:

Since at every movement an organism is within an environment which largely determines its behavior and since the environment changes - sometimes with radical abruptness - the conduct of an individual cannot be formulated without a characterization of each confronting situation, physical and social (39).

He also noted that socialization, defined as "the inculcation of culture patterns," played a role in personality development.   His concerns were with the relationship between environmental features and underlying needs of the individual (in Clausen, 1968:38).

A third theoretical focus in the personality work of the thirties was that of Kurt Lewin (1935) and his students.   His emphasis was upon the structure and press of the immediate situation.

A different area is that presented by Anderson (1936).   His work on The Young Child in the Home shows the pervasive influence of socioeconomioc status on child development and child rearing.

As can be seen from the represented works, the concern by psychologists has been how individuals change in specific contexts.

ANTHROPOLOGICAL VIEWS

"Developments within anthropology contributed more to the rise of interest in socialization in recent decades than did any other single influence" (Clausen, 1968:39).   One of the first works was Malinowsky's (1927) study among the Trobriand Islanders.   In another work, Sex and Repression in Savage Society (1927), the author was concerned with sequences of interaction and changing relationships required in the education of the child.

Mead in her study Coming of Age in Samoa (1928), used "education as a key concept to describe the process by which a newborn infant becomes a member of society; a member of his particular society and an individual in his own right" (41). In a personal communication to Clausen (1968), she noted that "socialization was not used as a technical concept until the mid-thirties" (41).

Sapir in 1927, for example, observed in "The Unconscious Patterning of Behavior in Society" that a great deal of patterned behavior results from the assimilation of linguistic forms, gestures, value orientations, and other cultural forms without clear awareness even of the existence of patterns (in Clausen, 1968:41-42).

As an anthropologist, Kardiner (1939) "was preoccupied with the imposition of infant-training, discipline and with the ways in which institutions interfere with impulses, relying heavily on psychoanalytic theory for his basic hypotheses. (He) postulated that the personality configurations produced by the 'primary institutions' were themselves responsible for the distinctive forms of folklore, mythology, and relation of the culture, which he termed 'secondary institutions.' This theoretical schema was to provide the model for the first efforts at quantitative cross-cultural research on socialization - the work of Whiting and Child" (1953; in Clausen, 1968:42-43).

A different approach to the study of socialization in a primitive society was John Whiting's Becoming a Kwoma (1941). His interest was in trying to explain the development of the Kwoma in terms of learning theory and thereby present a "theory of the process of socialization" (in Clausen, 1968:43).

Warner (1967), as another source of influence in anthropology and later in the field of human development, observed:

> It became clear to me that one needed not only to know about social structure at any given time, but one needed also to know about the psychic life of the individual and the changes going on in the psychic life of the individual, and then of course the relation of the growing individual to the changing society (in Clausen, 1968:43).

Clyde Kluckhohn (1939) noted:

> With a very few notable (and mainly recent) exceptions, anthropologists have failed to give systematic attention to the problem of how specific bits of culture are transmitted from individual to individual within particular societies. Such factual material as is available in the published literature is almost wholly anecdotal in character... A total conceptual scheme for attacking the question may be said to be nonexistent...
>
> I feel that it is fair to say that at the moment both the substantive and theoretical aspects of culturalization (if I may coin an admittedly horrid word) acutely need investigation (98)

He contributed markedly to systematizing and more adequately conceptualizing the process of socialization (in Clausen, 1968:44).

In summary, anthropologists have attempted to show how individuals acquire cultural characteristics and concurrently how the societies go about transmitting the necessary cultural characteristics. These two strands are similar to those theoretical developments in both psychology and sociology. What is very clear from this research is that the process of socialization is an interaction between individual and societal efforts. What is less clear is the variety of effects possible.

It can thus be seen that considerable specification of problems in the socialization process is provided. The aspects covered are individual characteristics, the content of preferred or required behavior to be acquired, and the process by which desirable content is transmitted, assimilated, and enacted. The critical characteristic of all of these studies is that the subjects studied have tended to be homogeneous and have been located in stable contexts. This has had certain consequences. First, the findings that have been reported in a continuing and consistent manner have not had relevance to heterogeneous populations or to populations which differ from those reported upon. Second, the neglect to report on heterogenous populations or on contrasting populations has provided limited information regarding the differing outcomes of socialization processes.

ROLE THEORY

Role theory has provided a means for explaining interpersonal relationships in several contexts. It has been most useful in providing a conceptual framework suitable for a discussion of personal interaction in organizations and institutionalized relationships such as those found in the professions, families, or classrooms.

Simmel (1895) was the first to employ social role as an analytical concept. The studies of "The Stranger" and "The Poor" as sociological types, which appear in his Sociology (1908) are prime examples of its use.

Other works, such as Katherine Lumpkin's (1933) The Family: A Study of Member Roles and G. H. Mead's (1934) Mind, Self, and Society followed. As an early contributor to role analysis, Mead brought out the fact that in a transaction the communication between parties is adequate only when each party puts himself into the role of the other. It is through taking the role of the other that a (a person) is able to come back on himself and so direct his own process of communication. Mead holds that the "ability of a person to take the role of another who is implicated with him in a transaction 'is not merely one of the various aspects of intelligence or of intelligent behavior but the very essence of its character... The whole nature of intelligence is social to the core'" (Mead, 1934:141).

Later, Jacob Moreno (1953) contributed the observation that role taking is faciliated by improvised role playing as a method of learning to perform roles more adequately. In his research he has shown that role playing, besides being important in socialization and acculturation, is also a significant therapeutic device (in Abel, 1974:201).

Contemporary studies of role phenomena in sociology were to a large extent prompted by Ralph Linton's (1936) linkage of social role with social status. "Status" is a term that specifies a position in a collective with its attendant right and duties and the rank that is assigned to it relative to other social positions. Status is preeminently an aspect of social structure. By proposing that role be viewed as the dynamic aspect of status, Linton established role performance as the missing link between individual behavior and social structure (Linton, 1936:113). Statuses are typically analyzed in terms of how they are interrelated to one another to form various types of social units (Turner, 1978:349-540). Since Linton, extensive research has been conducted using role as an analytical concept in the study of individual behavior in different social structures such as the educational system, the family, and the corporation. From these studies a number of theoretically significant formulations about general aspects of role performance have energed.

Herbert Blumer's (1969) brand of symbolic interactionism at one extreme through Kuhn's (1969) form of symbolic interaction, and then to Talcott Parsons' (1951) functional approach, emphasizing a highly structured image of status roles within institutionalized social systems, at the other extreme encompass a broad interactionist tradition in role theory. It is an eclectic theoretical tradition, with few dominant figures who have provided an overarching framework (Turner, 1978:347-348).

The thrust of the role perspective, as it flowed from Park (1939), Simmel (1895), Moreno (1953), Linton (1936), and G.H. Mead (1934) covers views drawn from players on the stage and actors in society. That is, the social world is viewed by role theorists as a network of variously interrelated positions or statuses, within which individuals enact roles. For each position, as well as for groups and classes of positions, various kinds of expectations about how incumbents are to behave are delineated.

Three general classes of expectations appear to typify role theory's vision of the world. 1) Expectations from the "script" - for many positions there are norms specifying just how an individual ought to behave. The conditions under which norms vary in terms of such variables as scope, power, efficacy, specificity, clarity, and degree of conflict with each other. 2) Expectations from other "players" - that is, role theory also focuses on the demands emitted by the other players" in the interaction situation. 3) Expectation from the "audience." These audiences can be real or imagined, constitute an actual group or social category, involve membership or simply a desire to be a member. As such, the audiences comprise a frame of reference or reference group that circumscribes the behavior of actors (Turner, 1978:350-351).

Individuals occupying positions and playing roles are typically conceptualized by role theory as revealing two interrelated attributes: a)self-related characteristics, and b) role-playing skills and capacities (Turner, 1978:352). This view roughly parallels Mead's (1934) portrayal of mind and self. That is, concern appears to be with the way individuals conform to what is expected of them by virtue of occupying a particular status. The degree and form of conformity are usually seen as the result of a variety of internal processes operating on individuals. Depending upon the interactive situation, these internal processes are conceptualized in terms of variables such as 1) the degree to which expectations have been internalized as a part of the individual's need structure, 2) the extent to which negative or positive sanctions are perceived by individuals to accompany a particular set of expectations, 3) the degree to which expectations are used as a yardstick for self-evaluation, and 4) the extent to which expectations represent either interpretations of others' actual reponse or merely anticipation of their potential responses (Turner, 1978:352-353).

Three basic emphases are present in role theory research. When conceptual emphasis is placed upon the expectations of individuals in statuses, then the special world is assumed to be composed of relatively clear-cut prescriptions. When conceptual emphasis falls upon the perceptions and interpretations of expectations, then the social world is conceived to be structured in terms of individuals' subjective assessment of the interaction situation. When conceptual priority is given to overt behavior, then the social world is viewed as a network of interrelated behaviors (Turner, 1978:354).

It appears, then, that role theory is concerned primarily with conceptualizing how different expectations emanating from different sources - norms, others, and reference groups - are mediated by self-interpretations and evaluations and circumscribed by role-playing skills in a way that a given style of role performance is evident. This style is subsequently typically analyzed in terms of its degree of conformity to expectations. However, at each stage in this sequence, certain "feedback" processes are also emphasized so that the degree of "significance" of norms, others, or reference groups for the maintenance of self-conceptions of individuals is considered critical in influencing which expectations are most likely to receive the most attention. Emphasis in this causal nexus is on the degree of imbeddedness of self in certain groups, the degree of intimacy with specific others, and the degree of commitment to, or internalization of, certain norms. Another prominent feedback process that has received considerable attention is the impact of overt behavior at one point in time on the expectations of others as they shape the individual's self-conception and subsequent role behavior at another point in time. In this context, the childhood and adult socialization of the individual and the emergence of self have extensively been studied, as has the analysis of the emergence of deviant behavior (Turner, 1978:356-357).

In regard to the interrelations among types of expectations, analytical attention appears to be on how specific "others" personify group norms or the standards of reference groups. In turn, these "significant" others are often viewed as deterministically linking the self-interpretations and evaluations of an individual to either the norms of a group or the standards of a reference group.

With respect to the relations among the components of self, analysis appears to have followed the lead of Williams James (1890;1948) by focusing on the connections between the "self-esteem" and the self-conceptions of an individual. Finally, all of these components interact in complex ways to shape the overt behavior of the individual (Turner, 1978:357).

Other developments of role theory by social psychologist and sociologists since the mid-40's have been persistent. Social psychologists (Ross and McDougall, 1908; Allport, 1924; Murphy and Murphy, 1937, Lewin, 1935; Moreno, 1953; Sarbin, 1954) have studied roles in relation to perception, to behavior, and to conflict, and of course, its contribution to the major task of establishing a theory of personality, or of the self (Turner, 1978:288).

Conceptual Development

Role Set

Sociologists have contributed to the study of roles by identifying some general features, as may be seen in the use of such terms as role-set, which R. R. Merton (1957) introduced to discuss the complex of relationships with a plurality of people or groups that a person, such as a school-teacher, may have, all making demands on him, some of which may be incompatible with others.

The general question about social mechanisms that regulate role performance was his concern (1957). He supplements Linton's (1936) observation that individuals occupy different statuses and therefore perform multiple roles with the observation that the single role a person plays in any one of the statuses he occupies is very frequently associated with multiple roles played by others. He cites the example of the single status of a medical student, which is connected with the role of his teachers, other students, nurses, physicians, medical technicians, and so forth. The multiple roles associated with the single status Merton calls a "role set" (Merton, 1957:369). A status can also be associated with other statuses and constitutes a "status-set," as Merton has pointed out. There are other permutations, for example, cases in which a single role is associated with multiple statuses or in which both roles are single.

Merton investigated the social mechanisms by which the roles constituting a role set become adjusted to each other. Such adjustment is necessary in view of the disturbance in a role set that might result from the fact that any person holding a particular social position is likely to have role partners who occupy different statuses and are ranked differently. Among these mechanisms Merton distinguishes those that help to promote differing degrees of involvement in the role relationship among the diverse people making up the role set or provide relative insulation of the occupant of a status from observation by some particpants in his role set.   The observability of members of the role set of their conflicting demands upon the occupant of a status also is a mechanism that allows him to "go his own way" while the other members of his role set are engaged in their conflict (Merton, 1957:377).

The process describing how expectations are fulfilled has been simplified by the use of the role set concept.   For example, it can be seen how interaction among the focal persons and the members of a role set is likely to stabilize over time, as expectations and reciprocal behavior contingencies become known.   Allport (1962); Kahn, et al. (1964), Evan (1966) and Weick(1969) have described this process as the development of a collective structure of behavior. Elaborating on the minimal social situation explored by Kelley (1955); Rabinowitz, et al. (1966) and Weick (1969), a necessary part of an analysis of organization is the consideration of the interlocking of individual behaviors.   When individual behaviors interlock with one another, uncertainty is reduced as the behaviors of the interlocked individuals become more predictable to each. Within an organization, members of the role set have expectations and preferences regarding the focal person's behavior.   These role expectations (Kahn, et al., 1964) may be communicated to the focal person, at which time they may become role pressures which potentially structure his behavior (141).

Pfeffer and Salancik (1975), in their study of supervisory behaviors, present a straightforward argument with the use of the role set concept.   Organizations are composed of interdependent positions and interlocking behavior.   Occupants of these positions are exposed to the expectations and social pressures of other organizational members with whom they are interdependent.   With experience, the expectations and demands become known, result in a collective structure of behavior, and stabilize to predictable patterns.   In any given position, the occupants's behavior is influenced and constrained by the social pressures emanating from other persons in his set (141).

Assuming that collective structures develop in organizations, Pfeffer and Salancik (1975) hypothesized that a supervisor's leadership behavior is influenced and constrained by the expectations of his subordinantes, his boss, and his peers. Moreover, the amount of constraints provided by each of these members of his role set is a function of the extent to which their behaviors interlock.   The supervisor, in this model, is not merely selecting that set of leadership behaviors that he prefers, or that he thinks will be best for him to use, but selects his behaviors subject to the social influences coming from his subordinates, his boss, and his peers and subject to their simultaneous selection of behaviors appropriate to interaction with him (141-142).

The researchers also expected that certain situational factors would affect the extent to which supervisory behaviors conform to the expectations of either bosses or subordinates.   Frequency of interaction (Weick,1969), the social similarity between the supervisor and those persons with whom he interacts, differences in authority among the parties involved, orientation to the demands of others, the number of persons supervised, and the work demands are the factors specified (Pfeffer and Salancik, 1975:145-146).

Their findings indicate that work of task-related supervisory activities in particular seem to be a function of the expectation of persons in the supervisor's role set. The greater the demands made by the supervisor's boss for the supervisor to produce the more the supervisor conformed in his work-related behaviors to the expectations of the boss, but there was no relationship between the demands made and the difference from subordinates' expectations of task-related behaviors. The greater the time spent supervising, the greater the conformity between the supervior's actual behavior and the supervisor's assessment of the boss's expectations for his behavior (Pfeffer and Salancik, 1975:150). Male supervisors engaged in behaviors that were closer to the expectations of their boss. The findings also indicated that female supervisors were less different in their work-related activities from the expectations of their subordinates. The larger the proportion of decisions made by the supervisor's boss, the more the supervisor differed from the subordinates' expectations, while conversely, the larger the proportion of decisions made by the subordinates, the less the supervisor differed from the work behavior of the subordinates.

Role Conflict

A significant exposure to role conflict, because of either role strain or disturbances in role set, has been linked by Parsons (1951) to social deviancy. In The Social System (1951), he sets forth the thesis that "exposure to conflicting expectations of some kinds may be presumed to be the generic situation underlying the development of ambivalent motivational structures with their expression in neurosis, in deviant behavior, or otherwise" (Parsons, 1951:282).

Other writings, many of them reviewed by Biddle and Thomas (1966), report on role conflict. Among the most prominent is Gross, Mason, and McEachern's study (1958) of school superintendents. These administrators' conflicts arise in their attempts to satisfy the often mutually exclusive desires of teachers, parents, and school board members. Similar dilemmas are presented in the experience of many women in modern society (Komarovsky, 1950). Foremen in industrial enterprises are also frequently "caught in the middle" between other workers, who perceive them as instruments of management, and management, which gives them little decision-making authorities" (Wray, 1949).

Two other concepts used in role conflict are the inter-role conflict and intra-work conflict. Inter-role conflict is primarily a function of the number of social roles held. Intra-work conflict is primarily a function of the position of the work role in the organization's structure and the role responsibilities (Herman and Gyllstrom, 1977:319). Herman and Gyllstrom found that the "academic professionals, whose positions interface in a service capacity with students and faculty - neither of which are known for their tact and patience -experience the   highest level of job tension. These are system boundary roles and the findings support those of Kahn et al, (1964) that people in boundary roles experience greater intra-role conflict than do those whose roles are more central to the system (332).

Role theory has also developed from studying persons whose roles are imprecise due to their social position placement. For example, Robert E. Park (1950) and Everett Stonequist (1937) wrote, regarding the marginal man, that when, through birth or other factors, individuals are placed between two not entirely compatible social positions, they may develop a distinctive set of personality characteristics.

Persons in such situations were described as manifesting their "double consciousness" by being ambivalent in sentiments and attitudes, sensing a divided loyalty, being moody, "irrational", and demonstrating some difficulty in inter-personal relationships. They are likely, according to the theory to be painfully self-conspicious, feel inadequate and excessively race-conscious, have feelings of impotence and inferiority, and to tend to withdraw socially. They were said to be hypercritical and contemptuous of those who occupy a lower status, have a certain skill at noting the hypocracies of those in super-ordinate positions, and as sometimes capable of perceiving and responding more creatively than those of homogeneous backgrounds. The advantages of marginality, however, were given little attention (Starr, 1977: 950-951).

Kerchhoff and McCormick (1955) reformulated the theory and delineated four major elements. These elements are: 1) the existence of a marginal status for a group, 2) the orientations of the individual members to their situation, 3) the level of rejection encountered by those who identify with and seek to join the dominant group, and 4) the psychological characteristics of marginal individuals (Starr, 1977 950-952).

Hughes (1949), applied the concept of marginality to those persons with a "status dilemma." They suffer a serious confusion about their roles and identities. This definition significantly broadened the category of potentially marginal persons, adding as variants those who have experienced extensive social mobility, occupy an ambiguous social status, or play a role with inherently contradictory elements.

This broader definition would potentially include a large number of persons in complex pluralistic societies. For example, many people in modern or rapidly changing societies are called upon to engage in behavior which involves contradictory obligations, or obligations which can shift sharply according to situational factors (Starr, 1977:953).

The enactment of a social role does not always conform strictly with the norms that regulate the expected conduct. William J.

Goode introduced the concept of role strain to denote the difficulties people experience in attempting to perform their role (Goode, 1960:483-496). He provided a typology of the sources of role strain, for example, role conflict as one source in cases when role expectations involve contradictory norms. One of his findings indicates that role strain is normal because the individual's total role obligations are overdemanding. But, he also showed that there are social mechanism at work that mitigate the strain so that it does not become disruptive. One of these is "role bargains" in which a person regulates his role performance by allocating claims for conformity made upon him by others in accordance with the role performance he can exact from them.

In summary, several discussions of marginality and role conflict have been presented. There are, however, in these studies certain theoretical, conceptual, and methodological problems. For example, investigations have often relied on descripitve techniques and have usually been concerned with small numbers of persons in limited situations. Some researchers considered a group as marginal or subject to role strain prior to starting their inquiry, assuming the phenomena to be present because the group in question fits into the existing broad, and somewhat elastic conceptualization. Many studies have not included "normal" or other control groups with which to compare responses. There is evidence in these studies that the conduct of individuals is influenced by conflicting group expectations, but the precise processes have not been specified.

In the present work, the contrast between the three groups: white males, women, and minorities demonstrates the difference organizational position placement can make in increasing or decreasing role conflict. For example, role conflict among white males as they assume administrative positions is lessened along various lines. First, they are socialized as teachers to enter administration Second, they are assigned to the vice-principalship as the entry level adminstrative position. During this time, they gradually learn to depart from children and instruction and assume administrative and managerial responsibilities. As their work demands increase, their perceptions about their work and themselves are altered in a compassionate environment. When they do assume the first "real" administrative position, the principalship, white males are prepared, so that role conflict may be non-existent.

In contrast to white males, women on the other hand, are more likely to move into positions such as the specialist. During this time they neither depart from children or instruction. They are granted greater access to adults, but because of their work demands, their perceptions about their work and themselves continue to include primacy to children and instruction. If they should be placed in an administrative position such as the principalship, role conflict is inevitable. They have not previously been prepared in adminstration or management. Neither have they learned that children and instruction are no longer primary concerns. Trying to fulfill incompatible demands women experience role conflict which may be perceived by other organizational participants as incompetency. Most seriously, women trying to be successful in their position resolve the role conflict by participating in a qualitatively different way from those of males. This ultimately results in women accentuating those role demands associated with administration and management. This behavior is subsequently viewed as defeminized and incompatible with normal perceptions of women. This may result in an increase in role conflict.

Minorities, as the third group being compared are also differentially placed in educational adminstration positions. They are found in special projects positions which continue to prepare minorities to deal with minorities and minority issues. It does not prepare them to depart from children and instruction. It does not prepare them to administer and manage adults and most seriously, insulates others within the organization from learning to deal with minorities and minority issues. When minorities are placed in administrative positions such as the principalship, they are usually placed in minority schools. This placement continues to relegate minorities to other minorities and fails to prepare them to administer and manage. For those minorities who do advance into the central office line positions, the potential of role conflict is managed by the manner in which they participate. They do not interfere in the white male's success arena and they do not compete with them. Instead, they serve to provide expertise in their area of ethnicity and on a social basis, they maintain graciousness and calm by synthesizing and integrating the white male's conversational material by witticisms, proverbs, and jokes.

As can be seen from the comparisons first presented, role conflict may be lessened, but also induced within an organizational setting by virtue of a person being placed in certain positions without adequate preparation. The point being made here is that it is possible to reduce role conflict in the assumption of important organizational positions. Most importantly, it is also demonstrated that efforts to reduce this conflict are concentrated on one group, white males, and not on women or minorities.

In summary, although accomplishing several empirical studies employing increasingly sophisticated methodologies, sociologists interested in the problem of status consistency have shown little concern with the theoretical aspects of the problem. Aside from Sampson (1963), Geshwender (1967) and Knabe (1972), few have considered the intervening processes between the occupation of inconsistent status and manifestation of various psychological predispositions (Starr, 1977:950).

Career Development

The study of roles has expanded to include a look at the establishment of careers. Several lines of research have developed. One of them is that exemplified in Hall's (1972) work. He defines a career "in terms of a person's changing identity over time" (Hall, 1972). Identity is generally defined as a person's perception of himself as he related to his environment. Miller (1973) has introduced the subidentity, which is useful to analyzing career growth. He refers to that aspect of the total identity engaged when a person is behaving in a given role (in Hall, 1972:472).

All subidentities have a certain area in common; this universal area is known as the core. Individuals can vary in different respects; number of sub-identities, degree of integration among subidentities (that is, size of the core), and congruence between subidentity and role (Hall, 1972:472). For example, married women's typical subidentities might be wife, mother, housewife, and employee.

Hall thinks of a career "as the series of personal changes a person experiences throughout the course of his or her life; an important aspect of these changes is identity change" (Hall, 1972:472). Career is used in its broadest sense, following Goffman's concept (1961) of the moral career and Hughes' notion (1937) of a subjective (versus objective) career. It refers to the unfolding process of a person's total life and need not refer only to occupational roles (Hughes, 1937).

Role Process

Following Levinson (1959), role is not defined as a unitary concept but rather as a process involving three components related to a person in given social positions: 1) structurally given demands, "norms, expectations, taboos, responsibilities...(and) sets of pressures and facilitations that channel, guide, impede, support (the person's) functioning...in one's positions;" 2) personal role conception, "inner definition of what someone in his social position is supposed to think and do about it;" and 3) role behavior, "ways in which members of a position act (with or without conscious intention) in accord with or in violation of a given set of organizational norms" (in Hall, 1972: 472-473).

This view is similar to the three events in the role process described by Kahn et al. (1964): role pressures communicated by other people, a person's experience of these pressures and his or her response. The role process, then, consists of a set of structural demands being placed upon the individual in a given social position. On the basis of both one's perception and one's own personality, a person formulates definition of what he or she should try to meet in his position. Based upon this personal definition, he/she decides how to behave (Kahn, 1964:473). In brief, the term role used in this manner serves as a concept covering the social position and its concomitant structural demands, personal role conception, and behavior (Hall, 1972:473).

Given the three levels of the role process: structurally imposed demands, personal role conception, and role behavior, coping mechanisms are derived which intervene in the role process at each level. First, the person can alter external, structurally imposed expectations held by others, regarding the appropriate behavior of a person in his or her position. This type of coping will be termed structural role redefinition, a strategy similar to Goode's concept (1960) of role bargain. One approach to coping would be to confront one's role senders and come to mutual agreement on a revised set of expectations (Hall, 1972:474).

Another way of changing structural demands would be to reallocate and share one's role tasks. The second type of coping involves changing one's personal concept of role demands received from others. This response is termed personal role redefinition. The third type of coping is reactive role behavior (Hall, 1972: 474).

An example of illustrating how this process works is the study by Athanassiades (1977). First, he concludes that the standard of the stereotype serves to structurally impose demands upon women's behavior. That is, women are publicly expected to be emotional, sociable, other-dependent, personable, and enthusiastically carrying on their daily chores (Althanassides, 1977:197). In contrast, women privately view themselves as self-centered, emotionally stable, willing to take risks, but also not enthusiastic about their present responsiblity. Finally, they respond by publicly presenting themselves as emotional, sociable, personable, and enthusiastically carrying about their daily chores. That is, women's public-selves are much closer to the female stereotype, rather than according to the dictates of the self-concept (Althanassiades, 1977:197).

There are, however, some women who don't respond in the manner described above. Those women "whose self-concept is higher than the female stereotype are less likely to conform to the stereotype" (197). They instead respond as they privately view themselves.

Two consequences result from those responses. The outward conformance of women to the prescription of the stereotype helps to perpetuate that stereotype (197-198). The second consequence is that more dynamic women, who don't conform to the stereotype, bear the burden of social sanctions for nonconformity. These sanctions take the form of unequal treatment, unequal opportunity, public disapproval and ridicule (198).

Another way to look at these consequences is that even when women conform, their treatment does not equalize, nor does their opportunity. Being considered emotional, dependent, and enthusiastically chore-complying is not particularly flattering.

What this role process indicates is that pervasive expectations serve to "shape" a person's behavior and that this mechanism is precise and identifiable.

Organizational Roles

One of the requirements of organizational functioning is patterned, predictable behavior (March and Simon, 1958; Thompson, 1967; Weick, 1969). Ideally, the roles of various organizational members are defined and structured in ways intended to assure behavior that contributes to the attainment of organizational goals. Therefore, individual behavior must somehow be induced or influenced to conform to role prescriptions (Kochan, et al., 1975:280).

Due to the organizational context, the transactional character of social relations involves a complementarity of roles rather than of persons. That is, the individuals in normatively regulated or institutionalized relations participate in them not as persons but as role performers or role takers. In this sense, the role being situationally determined and existing only by virtue of transaction, is not a psychlogical but a sociological concept (Abel, 1974:200).

Several important assumptions have guided the research in this area. Every person in a social group is influenced by expectations which others have of him. Some of these expectations may be highly formalized, as in a bureaucratic position description, or be less obvious and unarticulated. These expectations are disseminated throughout social groups and become internalized by individual members. Some of these expectations are congruent with one another, while others may be in conflict. These expectations may vary due to cultural, situational, or economic differences among individuals. When expectations among individuals are highly ambiguous or in conflict, interaction among those involved becomes strained. This problematic interaction, if extensive and prolonged, is incorporated into the self-image of the actors who experience it. The more often one is unable to satisfy the simultaneous expectations of others, and thereby come to anticipate some uncertainty in the behavior of others which can be expected in recurring situations, the greater the tendency for the actor to experience stress and a lowering of self-esteem. Conflicts in expectation may be "real", that is, refer to the actual expectations of others, or imagined, i.e., conflict is perceived by the actor, but his perception is not correct. With regard to the consequences for the individual concerned, however, the effect of either would be much the same. The conduct of others toward the actor is perceived as unpleasant or more negative than that initially anticipated by the actor. In an effort to avoid such stress and to raise self-esteem, the actor will pursue one or more alternatives. The easiest perceived means of reducing stress will tend to be selected before other alternatives. The tendency for stressful interaction to occur increases as the awareness of others increases regarding the discrepancy between their own expectations and the actor's attributes. If some discrepancies in expectations are limited to particular contexts which are avoidable, less visible, or more concealable than others, some forms of interaction will tend to be less stressful than others. There are no significant constraints operating, such as the pursuit of other rewards, to inhibit negative reactions on the part of others involved. There is no effective social support for the actor by other persons who share or who have shared the same situation or difficulties (Starr, 1977:957-958).

These assumptions are particularly useful in explaining the manner in which women and minorities participate in organizations. Using these assumptions as the basis for the analysis, it can be seen how in order to decrease stress between white males and women and minorities, they are placed in those organizational positions where interaction is lessened. Because rewards which would serve to minimize the impact of the stress are not available, the easier course is to route women to specialist, supervisory roles, and minorities to special projects roles rather than to regular line administrative positions.

The consequence is that few women and minorities are placed in organizational contexts where regular administrative roles may be actualized. But, as is shown in the present study, some women and some minorities do obtain and retain the regular line positions. Those who do, do not experience stress in their work due to conflicting work demands. Instead they occupy their positions because their personal preferences are to engage in that particular work with the positions' inherent work demands.

The stress which is present is that due to the organization's expectations regarding their ascribed roles such as being feminine or ethnic. Most seriously, the expectations are those arising from stereotyped cases. What is most pronounced in the present study is that the stress which occurs in educational administration participation is that all groups' perceptions about work demands and personal attributes are combined to create incompatibility between organizational positions and personal attributes. This continues in spite of women's and minorities' efforts to accentuate the positions' characteristics. It exists even if both women and minorities refuse to be shattered in the face of conflicting expectations.

What is indicated by the data presented in this work is that women and minorities actualize their organizational roles in a purer form without personal destruction. Nevertheless, there is an element of inequity in the degree of personal change which is required for women and minorities. There is also an element where the changes can occur in a more gradual manner. For example, women and minorities can be placed more often in the vice-principalship than they are.

By the same token, white males can be more equitably placed so that they occupy the specialist and supervisory positions in greater numbers than they presently do.

Toren (1974) states that:

> Modern role theory is based on the conception that a role is composed of several basic elements: a) the normative prescriptions defining how individuals occupying social positions are expected to behave; b) the perceptions of individuals of what they are supposed to do as incumbents or certain positions; c) role performance, or the actual behavior of individuals in given positions (101).

Multidimensional analysis that simultaneously treats various role components and their interrelation has only been rarely undertaken. Therefore, little is known about the way in which the norms, conceptions, and concrete actions pertaining to roles develop or change; the nature of the factors and processes affecting these different elements; or the conditions under which actual behavior is more likely to change and vary the norms of behavior (Homans,

1951; Dubin, 1959).

The study of groups of such women or minorities does provide a way for identifying those areas of behavior which do change as individuals occupy positions not normally occupied by members of their group.

One means is to analyze role in light of bureacratization. Bureaucratization is defined as the domination of the bureaucratic role over other roles of the incumbent and/or of those with whom he interacts. On the other hand, debureaucratization is the infringement of non-bureaucratic roles on bureaucratic ones (Katz and Eisenstadt, 1960), which modifies the neutrally - affective, specific, and universalistic nature of bureaucratic roles and role relationships. Thus, we would denote as debureaucratization the expression of feeling and emotion on the part of the official; the incursion of extrabureaucratic, or officially irrelevant roles and identities into his role relationships; the addition of tasks that extend the bureaucratic role beyond its specific boundaries; and 'special treatment' or a show of favoritism toward particular clients. Both directions of change - bureaucratization and debureaucratization - are deviations from the Weberian ideal-type bureaucracy in which the segregation of the official role from other social roles is strictly maintained (Weber, 1950:330-336; in Toren, 1973:202).

Katz and Eisenstadt (1960) in their study concluded that 'increased dependence of clients and officials on each other appears as a key factor' in the process of debureaucratization (118; in Torens, 1973: 110). This means that from the official's viewpoint "dependent" has a technical and social aspect. The technical element is generated by the need to count on the client to perform his role in accordance with certain established expectations. This aspect of dependence is a function of the degree of socialization and former experience of clients in bureaucratic role relationships. The social (or emotional) aspect is based on the official's need for sociability, friendliness, approval and the like, and is related to the degree of his insulation from colleagues and superiors (Torens, 1973:111).

This aspect is accentuated regarding women when they retain instruction and children in their work assignment. Similarly, this aspect is also present when minorities continue to direct and contain minorities through special projects administration.

Torens found that such dependence beyond the required instrumental and specific relations develops under conditions of danger (combat, work in the mines), unusualness of task (night shift), isolation from other social contacts and absence of the upper echelons of the bureaucratic hierarchy (men on a ship, or being in a distant rural community). Another factor which is likely to intensify the dependence of officials upon their clients and hence produce debureaucratization is prolonged and continual contact with the same clients. This enhanced their importance as sources of social and emotional gratification. (Torens, 1972:111).

Status and Conformity

Blau (1960) and Homans (1951) established that individuals of high status enjoy more leeway in regard to groups norms that those of middle status who are particularly disposed to be conformists. Homans explained this in his theoretical statement, "An increase of interaction between persons is accompanied by an increase of sentiments of liking and friendliness between them, (and) these sentiments will lead in turn to further interactions, over and above the interactions of the external system" (112).

Torens (1973) states that the "conception of role as a system composed of several elements, which are interdependent but not fully determined by each other, has furnished a viable and useful approach to role analysis." The examination of changes in role components (perception and performance) revealed that they were produced by different factors and tended to develop in different directions. The distinct patterns of perception were the result of the role incumbent's status in the organization, whereas different modes of role performance were related to the degree of continuity of contact with clients. In more general terms we may conclude, although tentatively, that actual behavior is likely to be affected by forces inherent in the situation of role performance, while perception tends to be influenced by factors outside this situation. The first part of the proposition is best illustrated by the way women and minorities adapt to the line positions. Women and minorities take into account the externally induced perceptions while they maximize their performance by attempting excellence and perfection. The latter part of this proposition is in accordance with the conclusion reached by Blau (1960) that a "worker's tendency to deviate from other members of his work group in his orientation to clients was not influenced by his experience, but it was related to his position in the group" (in Torens, 1973:110). What is evident from this research and the present study is that the official organizational role will not actualize under certain conditions.

Role Orientation

The writings of Levinson (1959) and Newcomb (1961) regard a person's own role definition (or 'role attitude') as an intervening variable between his official role prescription and his actual role performance. Merton's (1957) concept of 'social orientation' suggests that the underlying theme containing the sources and the characteristics of a person's role perceptions and performance might appropriately be called "role orientation" (Leopold, 1973:697).

Clues to more subtle types of social control are provided by reference group theory (Borgatta, 1959; Sherif, 1953; Shibutani, 1962). Contributions from these conceptual areas seem especially suitable to a study of representational behavior, since persons placed on community-wide boards and committees usually operate at a distance from their constituent groups (Leopold, 1973:699).

As stated before, prevailing views of role suggest that role performance depends not only on official role definition, but also on the personal interpretation the role-player attaches to it. A role consists of a set of norms which in any given situation guide individual behavior. Even without an explicit role prescription, a person acts according to certain external and internal cues. These correspond, respectively, to sent norms or the stable behavioral expectations emanating from a norm sender and received norms or the receiver's perceptions of certain expected norms. In the absence of an external role prescription, if the sent norms are ambiguous or contradictory, the individual presumably has a much wider choice of received norms than if a specific role expectation has been expressed (Leopold, 1973:699-700).

Reference group theory suggests how the source -or sources - of a person's role orientation may be identified, including those situations devoid of normative signals. Reference groups are defined as those groups to which the individual relates himself or to which he aspires to relate himself, psychologically. They are normative systems from which he derives his norms or that define the norms governing him in a specific situation. By focusing on internalized subjective norms for behavior rather than on external role prescriptions, reference group theory complements, and goes beyond, role theory (700).

A conceptual distinction must be made between ascribed and achieved status (Linton, 1936; Naegle, 1961) if unrealistic representative role expectations toward a specific group are to be avoided. A person may be perceived by others as holding a leading position or as identifying closely with a given group, when in reality this is not so. A representative appointment based on ascribed rather than achieved group status may thus be devoid of the usual normative controls described by reference group theory (Leopold, 1973:700).

Salience (Charters and Newcomb, 1958, Kelley, 1955) is another concept relating to sent and received norms. Salience is defined as the degree to which, in any given situation, a specific group is present in a person's awareness. In the current context, this suggests that situational reminders of the constituent group serve to heighten group-oriented behavior, regardless of whether or not the board member has been given a clear role prescription pertaining to that group (Leopold, 1973:700).

Finally, theorists dealing with the dynamics of group behavior suggest an important association between group interaction and group conformity (Bass, 1961; Blau and Scott, 1962; Cartwright and Zander, 1960; Etzioni, 1964; Gouldner, 1960; Hare, et al.,1955; Jackson, 1960; LaPierre, 1954; Roethlisberger and Dickson, 1939; Stogdill, 1959). Considered in conjunction with other factors believed to have a controlling effect on group members, variations in frequency, depth and formality of group interactions may help to explain the different degrees to which board members orient their board performance toward their respective constituent groups (Leopold, 1973:700-701).

142   CAREER PATTERNS IN EDUCATION

Other concepts derived from organizational theory aid in explaining delegation of authority, role prescriptions, and ways of influencing and controlling individual role performance (Barnard, 1938; Bernard, 1949; Beirstadt, 1954; Hopkins, 1961; Merton, 1957; Tannenbaum, 1962; Weber, 1947). For example, because an organization is a formal system of consciously coordinated activities by persons united in the pursuit of a common goal, in theory, at least, individual behavior in their organizations is determined and controlled by rigid role prescriptions for each organizational position (Leopold, 1973:699).

This is an important aspect to consider when examining the participation of women and minorities in educational administration. Sometimes it is perceived by some that individual women and minority administrators represent women and minorities. This perception justifies actions by superiors aimed at confining these individuals to their perceived groups' interests. The dysfunctional consequence is when the particular candidate and the group it represents expect the individuals to engage in administrative functions as do all other administrators.

As is indicated by the data, both women and minority line administrators acted according to a role orientation which was directed at administering and managing institutions. They did not view themselves as representatives of their respective groups. Nevertheless, they were keenly aware of others' perceptions regarding their group's stereotyped characteristics which were subsequently attributed to them on an individual basis.

Assimilation

Coulter and Taft (1973) state that:

The transition process involved in assimilation included such psychological factors as changes in attitudes and values; the acquistion of new social skills and behavior norms and consequent changes in role behavior; changes in reference group affiliation and group identification, and social and emotional adjustments to the new environment (in Leopold, 1973; 681).

A theoretical model advanced by Richardson (1961;1967) conceptualized the process of immigrant assimilation as being composed of three aspects, each of which follow each other as stages in a relatively unvarying sequence. The first stage is concerned with what happens to the immigrant during his initial period readjustment and resettlement. When the initial period of adjustment is successful, the immigrant may experience a general state of satisfaction with his new life, which is the foundation upon which his further assimililation rests. Provided that this state is attained, the conditions exist for the growth of an attachment or sense of belonging to the new community. Richardson (1961;1967) described this sense of belonging as the identification stage of the assimiliation process. He further asserted that to be so identified implies a favorable 'set' toward the host group, which is a condition under which the rapid adoption of its values, attitudes, and behaviour patterns may occur; that is, the immigrant achieves the acculturation state. Although Richardson (1961;1967) conceptualized assimilation as a unidimensional process comprising three sequentially-related stages, the theory does not imply that no identification or acculturation at all occurs until social and occupational needs have been completely satisfied. Some acculturation may occur in the absence of a high level of identification, and a moderate level of identification is possible in the absence of complete satisfaction (Richardson, 1961; 1967:681-682).

For example, Richardson (1961; 1967:683) writes that "in order to be fully assimilated to the teaching profession, a new teacher must enter the 'pedagogic culture' (Durkheim, 1956). This involves the adoption of appropriate attitudes, set of rules for one's behavior, and expectations for the behavior of others." Coulter and Taft's (1973) study:

> suggests that to concentrate on teaching a student the norms of his profession in the hope that this would increase his integration with it would be a mistake for those who are dissatisfied with their choice, or who have not started to become identified with the profession. Evidently, in the majority of cases, some degree of ego-involvement with teaching is needed before any convergence toward the norms of the profession is likely to occur (Richardson, 1967:692).

Role Shock

Minkler and Biller (1979) define role shock "as the stresses accompanying either major discrepancies between anticipated and encountered roles" or the sudden and significant departure from familiar roles which are "played differently" in the new setting or replaced altogether by new and unfamiliar roles. Its sources and manifest forms are described, with particular attention paid to the distinctions between role shock and the related concepts of culture shock, identity crisis, and such sociological constructs as role loss and role discontinuity (125).

Role shock experience is "viewed as a product of 1) the discrepancies between the anticipated nature of the unfamiliar role and the actual role encountered, or 2) the discovery that a major role change has occurred, where no such change had been anticipated" (127).

Role shock may be as critically linked with role leaving as it is with the taking on of a new role, particularly when the role one leaves behind is heavily bound up with his or her identity (Minkler and Biller, 1979:127).

Three major sources of role shock have been identified. These are: 1) changes in the relative "active" or "passive" nature of one's role, 2) critical discrepancies between anticipated and encountered roles, and 3) changes in the level of role ambiguity experienced by the actor. Each of these sources will now be described.

Changes in the "active" or "passive" natures of one's role is a major source of role shock. It is important to note, moreover, that it is not the directionality of the movement from either active or passive roles to their opposites, but rather the fact that critical, often unpredicted changes in either direction has occurred which creates the disruption (129).

Where roles are clearly defined and known before they are adopted, the subsequent discovery that things are not as they seemed may result in role shock (Minkler and Biller, 1979:130). In this case, role shock may occur within one's own familiar cultural setting (133).

A common behavioral manifestation of role shock among technical assistance workers has been described as the "retreat with professionalism" (131). For example, the loss of "all one's familiar cues" (Oberg, 1955:16) is replaced in role shock with the loss of cues specifically concerned with the ennactment of a specific role or group or roles (Minkler and Biller, 1979: 133).

The source of the disruption, in this case, lies not outside the individual but in a particular transactional exchange between a person and a society. The nonholistic nature of the exchange suggests that a selective set of role patterns must be unlearned and new ones acquired while the rest of one's world remains essentially the same (134).

Therefore, role changes giving rise to role shock may well result from voluntary and welcomed change of status, accompanied by increased prestige and responsibility, yet by the very fact of the change, still giving rise to severe tension and stress reaction.

The propensity for role shock in the movement through careers thus points up the need for easing the transitions both into and out of the work role, such that the "critical junctures of job entry, occupational change, unemployment, and retirement become less critical and thus less likely to involve major stresses and their sequelae" (Minkler and Biller, 1979:137).

In dealing with educational administration careers, it has been seen how the vice-principalship can serve as a position to reduce "role shock" as individuals depart from teaching, instruction, and children to enter administration, management, and adults. Women and minorities being denied access to the position would be expected to undergo some form of role shock.

Other types of role shock experiences predicated upon such events as sudden unemployment or retirement often are not cushioned by such symbolic passage validations and, consequently, the magnitude and nature of the tension and stresses observed may be somewhat of a different nature (137).

Role dispossession (Goffman, 1961) occurs when "meaningful roles are stripped away and not replaced by equally prestigious or desirable ones" (Minkler and Biller, 1979:163).

"Role continuity" (Benedict, 1938) suggests that, "under conditions of role continuity, training in one phase of cultural conditioning or socialization does not introduce one behavior while requiring a conflicting one later on, nor does it introduce behavior that has to be unlearned at some future date" (in Minkler and Biller, 1979:136).

"Role discontinuity," on the other hand, is the result of "conflicting or inconsistent standards, norm reversal, and unlearning (Minkler and Biller, 1979:136).

In summary, theoretical attention has not been given to certain areas. For example, role formation in broad social and pluralistic cultural structures has not been systematically studied. Ennacted role behaviors by contrasting groups and their effect on role-playing capacities have not been determined. The aspects dealing with enacted roles and the self-assessments that occur independently of role taking with specific others or groups have also been neglected.

Role Making

Ralph Turner's (1955) work dealt with role-taking and role-making. He stated that role-making can occur in three contexts: when individuals faced with only a loose cultural framework in which they must "make" a role to play; when they assume others are playing a role and thus "make" an effort to discover the underlying role behind a people's acts; when they seek to "make" a role for themselves in all social situations by emitting cues to others that give them claim on a particular role. This role-taking process as it becomes transformed into a role-making process is the underlying basis for all human interaction (372).

Turner argues further that in the process behavior is assessed not in terms of its "conformity" to imputed norms, but rather in regard to its "consistency" (372). Interaction is always a tentative process, a process of continuously testing the conception one has of the role of the other (in Turner, 1962:12).

Broadening the application of role theory, Turner (1978) states that pursuing a role, then, involves not only challenge from other role participants, but subtle influence from others which sharpens certain skills. By implication, given some initial desire to assume a specific role, one aspect of adequate socialization is the practical need to overcome differences among participants as means of sustaining motivation to learn that role (42).

It is in this manner that women and minorities, even though offered limited opportunities for successful socialization into the line administrative position, learn the requisite administrative role, fulfill the organizational expectations, and succeed as administrators. There is, however, a particular type of consequence. These processes are only possible to very few individuals.

CONCLUSIONS

In conclusion, it can be seen that both role and socialization theories lay the burden of successful organizational participation upon two critical elements. The individual's attributes or capacities and the organization's efforts. Both factors interact differentially in regard to the differing degrees to which both elements are present. That is, attributes and capacities are not equally present in all individuals. The efforts to aid individuals toward success in their organizational positions are also not equally exerted by the organization in relation to all individuals.

The contrast between three different groups in the present study shows that there are two aspects to an individual's attributes and capacities. The first is the actual presence and presentation of proof of the presence of attributes and capacities. The second is the perceived presence of attributes and capacities. These two aspects are critical in the examination of the manner by which women and minorities gain access to organizational positions.

The determination of the presence of attributes and capacities in an organizational setting is possible only in a very limited way. Special training and experience are two common means by which this occurs. For women and minorities, both means are problematic. However, in the case of educational administrtation, special training is more likely to be possible, since graduate and post-graduate programs are becoming readily available to them. Also, this training can be conducted outside the host organization. Another aspect to this is that the special training does not bind anyone to any actions.

Experience, on the other hand, is more problematic. This is critical to both women and minorities. Certain organizational skills, such as specific position technical skills and interpersonal skills, can only be acquired through the actual trial-and-error method. The acquisition of such skills is therefore confined to very specific settings and assignments. Proving the presence of such attributes and capacities is thus impossible unless an individual has had the opportunity to be actually placed in such settings. The point being raised here is that the determination of the presence of administrative attributes and capacities in women and minorities cannot be made without having women and minorities occupy certain organizational positions. Moreover, the acquisition and the develpment of additional attributes and capacities cannot take place without further occupation of specific educational administration positions. Instead, what is revealed in the present study is that the "perceived" attributes and capacities of women and minorities are used as the means for placing them in certain organizational positions and not in others.

The placement has two serious consquences. The first is that both women and minorities being excluded from administration and from intensive adult interaction are never able to display their capacities regarding technical or interpersonal skills. Moreover, being confined to instruction and children, they are never able to acquire the technical and interpersonal skills so critical to administration.

In regard to the second element, the organization's efforts to aid in the success of a person's participation, it can be seen in educational administration that partly due to the organization's perceptions about the three different groups, the organizations efforts are differential to them. This differentiation takes place in two different ways. First, in order to insure the successful career progression from teacher to superintendent, white males are provided opportunities in a sequential manner to master the requisite skills, attitudes, and knowledge as they advance. For example, one of the most traumatic periods for administrators is the transition between teacher and principal. White males are provided with the opportunity to occupy the vice-principalship. Women and minorities are less likely to occupy that position.

Second, not all positions offer the same experiences or opportunities to develop technical interpersonal skills. The line positions such as principal, assistant, associate, and deputy superintendent are positions which allow an individual to engage in activities which develop technical skills, such as school budgeting, and interpersonal skills, such as personnel administration. White males, occupying these positions, acquire these skills and ultimately become successful superintendents. Women and minorities, on the other hand, are not placed in these positions; therefore, these skills are not acquired. It can therefore be said that the organization does not try in an equitable manner to prepare individuals from the three groups to become superintendents. Instead it prepares white males to administer and manage adults, women to instruct children, and minorities to direct and contain other minorities. In this manner, the organization in failing to socialize women and minorites so that they have an equal oppportunity to attain the top position in educational administration.

The point being made and being supported by both role and socialization theories is that individuals by virtue of occupying certain positions in a specific sequence are either prepared to attain the superintendecy or not. More specifically, educational administration careers can be predicted by identifying the positions and the sequence by which they are occupied.

There is another consideration in this report. Those few women and minorities who were successful line administrators participated in a different manner from the rest. This is partly due to the fact that there are so few of them. Women are socialized in the company of males; minorities are socialized in the company of non-minorities. This context leads to differentiated socialization processes by virtue of the composition of the groups. This process would be different if the composition of the line officers in educational administration would be more heterogeneous.

Methodological Report

Data for the study reported upon were collected between September 1974 and April 1979. Most of the data were collected in Southern California school districts. However, some follow-up data collection extended to Northern California, Texas, and Arizona.

The method for data collection was ethnographic. Extensive observation of school sites, administrators at work, meetings, informal gatherings and other settings was conducted. Interview data were collected from 350 schools administrators. Administrators were defined as those who were occupying school positions which required the California State Administrative Credential.

The school administrators consisted of 127 women, 223 men; 55 Hispanic women, 17 Black women, 20 Hispanic men, 15 Black men, 55 white women, and 188 white men. The various positions represented were: 15 vice pricipals, 82 elementary principals, 69 secondary principals, 22 directors, 3 coordinators, 8 specialist, 8 supervisors, 27 special projects coordinators, 21 special projects specialists, 12 special projects supervisors, 2 area administrators, 17 associate superintendents, 22 assistant superintendents, 23 deputy superintendent and 20 superintendents.

Interview data were also collected from other school personnel. A total of 48 persons were interviewed consisting of 7 school board members, 8 parents, 2 teacher aids, 2 secretaries and 29 teachers. Five conversational reports with students were also included.

Thirty-one school districts are represented. The reason for this extensive coverage is that as subjects were located according to position, their placement was in any number of school districts. The districts ranged in size from enrollments of 2893 to 721,043. All of the school districts which are represented contain a central office.

The inspection of documents provided information regarding official job descriptions and expectations. Other written materials included personnel directories, listings, vacany notices and proposals for various programs.

The study began with its focus on career patterns among school administrators. Data were initially collected by interview. As the data were accumulated and the first level of analysis was conducted, it appeared that certain educational administration positions provided more opportunities for movement than others.

The direction of the research, then shifted to determine differences between educational administration positions.

This turn of events required several changes. First, observation of positions was deemed important. Second, interview schedules became more open-ended. Third, the selection of subjects became that of locating positions and certain types of persons such as women and minorities. This resulted in expanding the number of school districts in order to find women and minorities in the executive educational positions. Much of this work was carried out by inspecting school directories and other listings to insure coverage of differently titled positions.

As stated previously, this sample was derived as a result of the direction of the research The first batch of subjects consisted of senior school administrators, high school principals, associate, assistant and deputy superintendents drawn from 12 Southern California school districts.

When the decision was made to differentiate school administration positions, the list was expanded to include vice-principals, specialists, coordinators and various other positions under "special projects," and area administrators.

As subjects were being drawn to correspond to the final list, it was noted that position holders couldn't be readily located in some of the positions. For example, locating white male specialists was problematic. Another issue which arose was locating minorities in the various positions. For example, locating Hispanic female secondary principals was difficult. This last factor led to expanding the data gathering area to include the Greater Los Angeles Metropolitan Area.

Another decision which was made by the researcher was to place special emphasis on Hispanic female school administrators. This was based partly on a study being carried on at the same time by Dr. Yolanda Venegas in which she surveyed a total of 46 Chicana school administrators in the Greater Los Anglese Area (see Ortiz and Venegas, 1978). From this experience the paucity of literature dealing with this group was realized. More seriously, the sparse placement of Hispanic women in school districts was noted. Using the survey and follow-up data from this group. the sample was expanded to include Hispanic school adminstrators from small and medium sized school districts. A total of nine Hispanic females was located.   This study therefore, reports on a total of 55 Hispanic female school administrators.

The composition of the total data pool consisted of 15 vice-principals, 82 elementary principals, 69 secondary principals, 22 directors, 3 coordinators, 8 specialists, 8 supervisors, 27 speical projects coordinators, 21 special projects specialists, 12 special projects supervisors, 2 area administrators, 17 associate superintendents, 22 assistant superintendents, 23 deputy superintendents, and 20 superintendents.

The inspection of documents also provided information regarding official job descriptions and expectations. In several cases the career movement of individuals could also be traced by examining directories, personnel listings, vacancy notices, and proposals for various programs. For example, the position of area administrator was noted to be referred to as area superintendent by the organizational participants, but was listed on all official documents as area administrator. A further investigation showed that the description of the position, the acquisition, and the day-to-day expectations of the positions were different. Several districts had made these changes during the mid-sixties and early seventites. Therefore, the review and analysis of documents served to verify and clarify interview and observational data.

During the course of the study, many subjects were promoted, demoted, or transferred. Those districts not represented in the initial pool of data were not included among the 31 districts. Movement of school administrators during the five-year period included movement to other school districts throughout California. One person left to Arizona and another to Texas.

An unforseen benefit of the long-term data collection period was the opportunity to see individuals promoted to positions which otherwise were not occupied by those particular groups. For example, a woman associate superin-tendent became a superintendent during the period of the study. Also several minorities were promoted from lower administrative posts to the assistant superintendency and superintendecy posts. This provided a means for including within the sample a more varied representation of the available educational administration positions. Most importantly, it provided a means for strengthening the argument that some positions contain propelling characteristics while others do not. These characteristics are more obvious where it concerns women and minorities.

The total number of school districts involved and the total number of changes during the period of study are summarized in Tables 7-12.

The present study was not conducted without serious involvement. The researcher had begun the investigation with the intention to discover how school careers were established in order to provide an explanation for the absence of women and minorities in certain positions and not in others. Because the characteristics of the positions emerged as powerful indicators of organizational participation and movement, the researcher focused on this aspect more than on others. This had certain methodological consequences.

First, it required intensive observation of some positions and not others. This sometimes called for an explanation to school officials. Second, special observation emphasis was placed on those positions which were occupied as a result of advancement during the period of study. For example, when Hispanic females were newly appointed an intense observational schedule was attempted. This was sometimes problematic for both the candidate and the organization. Individuals would quest on why these persons were being observed so closely. On two of these occasions, the observer did not complete the scheduled observation. Data were gathered instead by interview and documents such as job descriptions, memos, daily logs recording telephone calls and visitors, and organizational calendars.

Several limitations were placed upon the data collection for this report. First, observation of newly appointed minority persons was incomplete. Second, interview data were deleted because they were later recalled by an associate superintendent because he felt it might be damaging to the individuals involved and the organization. All data related to this incident, position, and position holders were withdrawm from the data pool. Third, incomplete interview data collected from two position holders which could be not be verified were deleted. Fourth, follow-up data collected through the telephone from six position holders is included. All of these persons had moved from the area and the data were thus collected in this manner. Fifth, data collected through correspondence from one position holder is included. The person had moved and contact was established by mail. The person responded to some direct question regarding changes in position.

The process in the analysis of the data is highly personal. This researcher admits that the preoccupation with position differences in organizations is based on experiences and insights which have guided this investigation. But as Shils (1961:1405-50) writes:

> Sociological analysis, however much we succeed in systemizing, codifying, routinizing it – however close we bring it to the natural sciences in rigor of procedures, in the reliability of observation, and in the refinement of demonstration – will always retain an important element of the personal. By this, we mean that the most elementary categories, the most fundamental variables, will have to be apprehended through an experience, through a kind of secular revelation. The operational definition of terms will be useful in the design of research; but what is defined will never be learned from handbooks, nor will it be learned ordinarily from the study of concrete investigations. The best sociological theory will encompass these variables; but the theory itself will need the guidance of the "experience" or of the vision, of authority, and the refusal of order, of scarcity, of loving attachment, and of hatred. Even the possible mathematization of sociological theory will not evade this necessity or recurrent refreshment of the experience of the fundamental variables of sociological theory. The fundamental terms of sociological theory are primitive terms. Their meanings are apprehended in personal experience and through the secondary experience of contact with the vision, which expresses the deepest experiences of the greatest minds of the race (1148).

The study's analysis, therefore, was developed with concepts and social categories which were particularly attractive to this researcher. The data were ordered in accordance to the logic as perceived by this researcher. Educational administration, nevertheless, remains to be investigated in varied ways by different methods to be more fully understood.

TABLE 7. School District Enrollment Size

District	Enrollment	District	Enrollment
A	2,893	Q	15,262
B	5,626	R	17,016
C	5,795	S	17,420
D	6,000	T	18,124
E	6,716	U	20,391
F	7,227	V	23,682
G	8,977	W	23,862
H	10,039	X	25,500
I	10,745	Y	25,814
J	10,797	Z	26,703
K	10,847	AA	29,367
L	11,624	BB	30,944
M	11,689	CC	32,186
N	11,754	DD	32,480
O	13,017	EE	721,043
P	13,683		

TABLE 8.   Educational Administration Position Occupancy

Vice-Principals	Elementary Principals	Mid-High Principals
4 white female	16 Hispanic female	3 Hispanic female
11 white male	5 Hispanic male	2 Hispanic male
15	4 Black female	5 Black female
	2 Black male	1 Black male
	17 white female	5 white female
	38 white male	17 white male
	82	33

High School Principals	Directors	Special Projects Directors
2 Hispanic male	1 white female	8 Hispanic male
1 Black female	5 white male	8 Black male
2 Black male	6	16
2 white female		
29 white male		
36		

Coordinators	Specialists	Supervisors
3 white male	2 Hispanic female	4 white female
	1 Black female	4 white male
	2 white male	8
	3 white female	
	8	

Special Projects Coordinators	Special Projects Specialists	Special Projects Supervisors
20 Hispanic female	10 Hispanic female	4 Hispanic female
2 Black female	3 Black female	1 Black female
4 white female	6 white female	4 white female
26	2 white male	3 white male
	21	12

Area Administrators	Assistant Superintendents	Associate Superintendents
2 Black male	2 white female	2 white female
	20 white male	15 white male
	22	17

Deputy Superintendents	Superintendents	
1 white female	3 Hispanic male	
22 white male	17 white male	
23	20	

TABLE 9.   Position Changes Among School Administrators

Number	Initial Position	Position Moved To	
20	Superintendents	2 Federal posts 2 State posts 2 University posts	3 Retired 1 Unaccounted 10 Remained
17	Associate superintendents	4 Superintendents 1 State post 1 Unaccounted 11 remained	
22	Assistant superintendents	1 University post 3 Unaccounted 14 remained	2 Superintendents 1 Associate superintendent 1 Deputy superintendent
23	Deputy superintendents	2 Unaccounted 17 remained 1 Federal post	1 Superintendent 2 Associated superintendents
36	High School principals	2 left 2 Unaccounted 21 remained 1 back to classroom	2 Superintendents 7 Assistant superin- tendents 1 Director of special projects
33	Mid-high principals	1 Area administrator 2 back to classroom 1 left 1 Unaccounted 19 remained 2 High school principals 1 Elementary principal	1 Director 1 Director of special projects 4 Assistant superinten- dents
82	Elementary principals	2 mid-high principals 1 Director of special projects 3 Special projects coordinators 1 Special projects supervisor 3 moved 2 Unaccounted	3 Coordinators 1 Specialist 5 back to classroom 2 left school district 1 left educa- tion 58 remained

TABLE 10. Career Movement Among White Men

Number	Initial Position	Position Moved To
11	Vice-principals	3 High school principals 1 left 5 Elementary principals 2 back to classroom
38	Elementary principals	2 Coordinators 1 Mid-high principal 1 left school 2 back to classroom district 2 Unaccounted 30 remained
17	Mid-high principals	1 Director 2 High school 1 back to classroom principals 1 left district 1 Assistant 1 Unaccounted superintendent 10 remained
29	High School principals	2 left 1 Superintendent 2 Unaccounted 3 Assistant superin- 20 remained tendents 1 back to classroom
5	Directors	1 Assistant superintendent 1 Coordinator 1 State post 2 remained
15	Associate superintendents	3 Superintendents 1 Unaccounted 1 State post 10 remained
20	Assistant superintendents	2 Superintendents 1 University post 1 Deputy superintendent 3 Unaccounted 1 Associate superintendent 12 remained
22	Deputy superintendents	2 Unaccounted 1 Superintendent 16 remained 2 Associated 1 Federal post superintendents
2	Specialists	5 remained
4	Supervisors	1 Coordinator 1 back to classroom 2 remained
2	Special projects specialists	1 remained 1 State post
3	Special projects supervisors	1 Director 1 remained 1 Unaccounted
3	Coordinators	1 Unaccounted 2 remained
17	Superintendents	1 Federal post 3 Retired 1 State posts 1 Unaccounted 2 University posts 9 Remained

TABLE 11. Career Movement Among White Women

Number	Initial Position	Position Moved To
4	Vice-principals	2 Elementary principals 1 High school principal 2 back to classroom
17	Elementary principals	1 Coordinator 1 left school district 1 back to classroom 14 remained
5	Mid-high principals	1 Assistant superintendent 4 remained
2	High School principals	1 remained 1 Assistant superintendent
2	Associate superintendents	1 Superintendent 1 remained
2	Assistant superintendents	2 remained
1	Deputy superintendents	1 remained
1	Directors	1 Assistant superintendent
3	Specialists	1 Supervisor 2 remained
4	Supervisors	1 Coordinator 3 remained
4	Special projects coordinators	1 left school district 3 remained
6	Special projects specialists	4 remained 1 left school district 1 Special projects supervisor
4	Special projects supervisors	1 Director of Special projects 2 remained 1 Unaccounted
22	Deputy superintendent	1 Superintendent 2 Associate superintendents 1 Federal post 2 Unaccounted 16 remained
2	Specialists	2 remained
4	Supervisors	1 Coordinator 1 back to classroom 2 remained
2	Special projects specialists	1 remained 1 State post
3	Special projects supervisors	1 Director 1 remained 1 Unaccounted
3	Coordinators	1 Unaccounted 2 remained
17	Superintendents	1 Federal post 3 Retired 1 State posts 1 Unaccounted 2 University posts 9 Remained

TABLE 12. Career Movement Among Minorities

Number	Initial Position	Position Moved To
27	Elementary principals	1 Director of Special Projects 1 Special Projects Director 3 Special Projects Coordinators 2 Mid-high principals 1 left educatio 2 back to classroom 14 remained 3 moved
11	Mid-high principals	1 Area administrator 1 Elementary 2 back to classroom principal 4 remained 2 Assistant 1 Director of superintendents Special Projects
5	High School principals	1 Superintendent 1 Director Special Projects 3 Assistant Superintendents
16	Special Projects Directors	3 Assistant Superintendents 2 Elementary Principals 1 Unaccounted 10 remained
3	Specialists	1 remained 1 Supervisor 1 back to classroom
22	Special Projects Coordinators	1 Director 1 Supervisor 1 left district 1 Unaccounted 18 remained
13	Special projects Specialists	11 remained 1 Special Projects Supervisor 1 Special Projects Coordinator
5	Special projects supervisors	1 Special Projects Coordinator 3 remained 1 Elementary Principal
2	Area Administrators	2 remained
3	Superintendents	1 Federal post 1 State post 1 remained

References

Abel, Theodore, "The Operation Called Vestehen," In Truzzi, Marcello, (ed.), Vestehen: Subjective Understanding in the Social Sciences, Reading, Mass.: Addison-Wesley and Co. 1974.

Allport, F.H., "A Structuronomic Conception of Behavior: Individual and Collective, Journal of Abnormal and Social Psycholgogy, 64 (1962), 3-30.

Allport, F.H., Social Psychology, New York: Houghton-Mifflin Co., 1924.

American Association of School Administrators (AASA), Profile of the School Superintendent, Washington, D.C.: American Association of School Administrators, 1960.

American Association of School Administrators, Thirty-Third Yearbook, Staff Relations in School Administration, Washington, D.C., February, 1955, 22.

Anderson, J.E., The Young Child in the Home: A Survey of Three Thousand American Families, Report of the Committee on the Infant and Preschool Child, White House Conference on Child Health and Protection, New York: Appleton-Century, 1936.

Althanassiades, John C. "The Internalization of the Female Stereotype by College Women," Human Relations, 30, 2 (1977), 187-199.

Baldwin, J.M., History of Psychology, Vol.2, New York: Putnam, 1913a.

Baldwin, J.M., The Individual and Society, Boston: Richard Badger, The Gorham Press, 1911.

Banton, Michael P. , Roles: An Introduction to the Study of Social Relations, New York: Basic Books, 1965.

Barnard, ChesterI., The Functions of the Executive, Cambridge, Mass: Harvard University Press, 1938.

Bass, B., "Conformity, Deviation and a General Theory of Interpersonal Behavior," in Berg, I. and Bass, B. (eds.), Conformity and Deviation, New York: Harper & Bros., 1961.

Becker, Howard S., "The Career of the Chicago Public School Teacher," American Journal of Sociology, 57 (March, 1952), 470-477.

_____, "The Elements of Identification With an Occupation," American Sociological Review, 21 (June, 1956), 341-348.

_____, "The Nature of a Profession," In Education for the Professions, Sixty-First Yearbook of the National Society for the Study of Education, Chicago: University of Chicago Press for the Society, 1962, 27-46.

_____, "Personal Change in Adult Life," Sociometry, 27 (March, 1964), 40-53.

_____, and James W. Carper, "The Development of the Identification with an Occupation," American Journal of Sociology, 61 (January, 1956), 289-298.

Benedict, Ruth, "Continuities and Discontinuities in Cultural Conditioning," Psychiatry, 1 (1938), 611-617.

Benedict, Ruth, Patterns of Culture, Boston: Houghton-Mifflin Co., 1934.

Bernard, J., American Community Behavior, New York: The Dryden Press, 1949.

Biddle, B.J. and Thomas, E.J. (eds.), Role Theory: Concepts and Research, New York: Wiley, 1966.

Bierstadt, R. "The Problem of Authority," in Berger, M., Abel T., and Page, G. (eds.),Freedom and Control in Modern Society, New York: D. Van Nostrand Co., Inc., 1954.

Blau, P.M. "Patterns of Deviation in Work Groups," Sociometry, 23 (1960), 245-261.

Blau, P. and Scott, R., Formal Organizations: A Comparative Approach, San Francisco: Chandler Publishing Co., 1962.

Blood, Ronald E., The Functions of Experience in Professional Preparation: Teaching and the Principalship, Unpublished doctoral dissertation, Claremont Graduate School, Claremont, California, 1966.

Blumer, Herbert, Symbolic Interactionism: Perspectives and Method, Englewood Cliffs, N.J.: Prentice-Hall, Inc., 1969.

Borgatta, E., "Role and Reference Group Theory," in Kagan, L., (ed.), Social Science Theory and Social Work Research, Proceedings of an Institute held by the social work research section of the National Association of Social Workers, June 1959, New York: National Association of Social Workers, 1960.

Boskoff, Alvin, The Mosaic of Sociological Theory, New York: Thomas Y. Crowell Co., 1972.

Bridges, Edwin M., "Bureaucratic Role and Socialization: The Influence of Experience on the Elementary Principal," Educational Administration Quarterly, 1 (1965), 19-28.

Brim, Orville G., Jr., "Adult Socialization," from John A. Clausen, (ed.), Socialization and Society, Boston: Little, Brown & Co., 1968, 182-226.

_____, and Wheeler, S., Socialization After Childhood: Two Essays, New York: John Wiley & Sons, 1966.

Briner, Conrad and Laurence Iannaccone, "Selected Social Power Relationships in Education," Educational Administration Quarterly, 3 (Autumn 1966), 190-202.

Burgess, Ernest W., The Function of Socialization in Social Evolution, Chicago: University of Chicago Press, 1916.

California Public School Directory, Sacramento: California State Department of Education, 1975.

California Public School Directory, Sacramento: California State Department of Education, 1979.

Caplow, Theodore, The Sociology of Work, Minneapolis: University of Minnesota Press, 1954.

Carlson, Richard O., Executive Succession and Organizational Change, Chicago: University of Chicago, Midwest Administration Center, 1962.

_____, School Superintendents: Careers and Performance, Columbus, Ohio: Merrill, 1972.

_____, "Succession and Performance Among School Superintendents," Administrative Science Quarterly, 6 (1961), 210-227.

Cartwright, D. and Zander, A. (eds.), Group Dynamics: Research and Theory, New York: Harper & Row, 1960.

Casso, Henry J., "Higher Education and the Mexican-American," In Tyler, Gus, (ed.), Mexican-Americans Tomorrow: Educational and Economic Perspective, New York: Weatherhead Foundation, 1975, 137-163.

Charters, W.W., Jr., "An Approach to the Formal Organization of the School," In Griffiths, Daniel E., (ed.), National Society for the Study of Education, Behavioral Science and Educational Administration, Chicago: University of Chicago, 1964, 243-261.

Charters, W. and Newcomb, T., "Some Attitudinal Effects of Experimentally Increased Salience of A Membership Group," In Maccoby, E., Newcomb, T., and Hartley, E. (eds.), Readings in Social Psychology, New York: Henry Holt & Co., 1958.

Child, I.L., "Socialization," In Linzey, G., (ed.), The Handbook of Social Psychology, Cambridge, Mass.: Addison-Wesley Publishing Co., 1954, 655-692.

Clausen, John A., (ed.), Socialization and Society, Boston: Little, Brown & Co., 1968.

Cohen, Michael D. and James G. March, Leadership and Ambiguity, New York: McGraw-Hill Book Co., 1974.

Colombutos, John, Sources of Professionalism: A Study of High School Teachers, Washington, D.C.: U.S. Government Printing Office, 1962.

Contreras, A. Reynaldo, "Spanish-Surnamed Administrators," Emergent leadership, 3, 2 (Spring,1979), 33-47.

Cooley, C.H., Human Nature and the Social Order, New York: Scribner's, 1902, Rev. Ed., 1922.

Corwin, Ronald G., A Sociology of Education, New York: Appleton-Century-Crofts, 1965.

Coulter, Frank and Ronald Taft, "The Professional Socialization of School Teachers as Social Assimilation," Human Relations, 26, 2 (1973), 681-693.

Covel, Janice M. Analysis of School Administrators' Careers in Riverside County From 1870-71 to 1974-75, Unpublished Dissertation, University of California, Riverside, California 1977.

Dewey, J., Human Nature and Conduct, New York: Holt, 1922 or Modern Library Education, 1930.

Dils, Eugene, "How Administrators Climb the Ladder," The School Executive, 74 (September, 1954), 62-63.

Dollard, J., "Culture, Society Impulse, and Socialization," American Journal of Sociology, 45 (1939), 50-63.

Dreeben, Robert, "The School as a Workplace," in Travers, Robert, M. W., (ed.), "Second Handbook of Research on Teaching, Chicago: Rand McNally College Publishing Co., 1973.

Drust, Bess, Factors Related to the Employment of Women as Junior High School Principals, Assistant Superintendents, and Superintendents in California Public Schools, Unpublished doctoral dissertation, Brigham Yong University, 1976.

Dubin, R., "Deviant Behavior and Social Structure," American Sociological Review, 24 (1959), 147-164.

Durkheim, E., Education and Sociology, Glencoe, Ill.: The Free Press, 1956.

Elkin, F., The Child and Society: The Process of Socialization, New York: Random House, 1960.

Equal Employment Opportunity Commission, Employment Opportunity in the Schools: Job Patterns of Minorities and Women In Public Elementary and Secondary Schools, Washington, D.C.: U.S. Government Printing Office, 1977.

Etzioni, Amitai, "Authority Structure and Organizational Effectiveness," Administrative Science Quarterly, 4 (June, 1959), 43-67.

_____, Complex Organizations - A Sociological Reader, New York: Holt, Rinehardt and Winston, Inc., 1961.

Evan, W.M., "The Organization Set: Toward a Theory of Interorganizational Relations,"In Thompson,J.D., (ed.), Approaches to Organizational Design, Pittsburgh: University of Pittsburgh Press, 1966.

Fishel, Andrew and Pottker, Janice, "Women Teachers and Teacher Power," Urban Review, 6, 2 (November-December, 1972), 40-44.

Foote,   N.N.   and   Cottrell,   L.S.,   Jr.,   Identity   and Interpersonal Competence: A   New   Direction   in   Family Research, Chicago: University of Chicago Press, 1955.

Friedricks, Robert Winslow, A Sociology of Sociology, New York: Free Press, 1970.

Fromm, Eric, Escape from Freedom, New York: Farrar & Rinehart, 1941.

Fromm, Eric,   The Sane Society, New York: Rinehart, 1955.

Geschwender,   J.A.,   "Continuities   in   Theories   of   Status Consistency   and   Cognitive   Dissonance,"   Social   Forces,   46 (1967), 167-179.

Giddings, F.P., The Theory of Socialization, New York: The Macmillan Co., 1897.

Gittell,   Marilyn,   Participants   and   Participation: A   Study   of School   Policy   in   New   York   City,   New   York: Frederick   A. Praeger Publishers, 1967.

Glaser,   Barney   G.,   Organizational   Scientists: Their Professional Careers, Indianapolis: The Bobbs-Merrill   Co., Inc., 1964.

Goffman, E., Asylums, New York: Doubleday, 1961.

Goode, W.J., "Theory of Role Strain," American Sociological Review, 25 (1960), 483-496.

Gouldner,   A.,   "Organizational   Analysis,"   In   Kagan,   L.   (ed.), Social Science Theory and Social Work Research, Proceedings of an institute held by the Social Work research section of the National Association of Social Workers, June 1959, New York: National Association of Social Workers, 1960.

Greabell, Leon C., and John A. Olson, "Role Dissatisfaction and Career   Contingencies   Among   Female   Elementary   Teachers," Journal of Spate, 11,4 (June 1973), 131-138.

Greenleaf, Elizabeth A., "The Role of Women in Education: Responsiblilty of Educated Women," Educational Horizons, 52, 2 (Winter, 1973-74), 77-81.

Griffiths, Daniel E., The School Superintendent, New York: The Center for Applied Research in Education, Inc., 1966.

Griffiths, Daniel E., Goldman, S., and McFarland, W.J., "Teacher Mobility in New York City," Educational Administration Quarterly, 1 (1965), 15-31.

Gross, Neal, Mason, W.S., and McEachern, A.W., Explorations in Role Analysis: Studies of the School Superintendency Role, New York: Wiley, 1958.

_____, Trask, Ann E., The Sex Factor and the Management of Schools, New York: John Wiley and Sons, 1976.

Hall, Douglas T., "A Model of Coping With Role Conflict; The Role Behavior of College Educated Women," Administrative Science Quarterly, 17, 4 (December, 1972), 471-486.

Halpin, Andrew W., The Leadership Behavior of School Superintendents, Columbus, Ohio: Ohio State University Press, 1950.

Hare, A.P., Borgatta, E., and Bales, R. (eds.), Small Groups: Studies in Social Interaction, New York: Alfred A. Knopf, 1955.

Hemphill, John K., Griffiths, Daniel E., and Frederickson, Norman, Administrative Performance and Personality, New York: Bureau of Publications, Teachers College, Columbia University, 1962.

_____, John K. Richards, James M., and Peterson, Richard E., Report of the Senior High School Principal, Washington, D.C.: The National Association of Secondary-School Principals, 1965.

Herman, Jeanne Brett and Gyllstrom, Karen Kuczynski, "Working Men and Women: Inter and Intra Role Conflict," Psychology of Women Quarterly, 1, 4 (Summer 1977), 319-333.

Himmelweit, Hilde T. and Sealy, A.P., "The School as an Agent of Socialization," London, 1966 (Mimeo).

Homans, G.C., The Human Group, London: Routledge and Kegan Paul, 1951.

Hopkins, T., "Bureaucratic Authority: The Convergence of Weber and Barnard," In Etzioni, A. (ed.), Complex Organizations: A Sociological Reader, New York: Holt, Rinehart and Winston, Inc., 1961.

Hughes, Everett C., "Institutional Office and the Person," American Journal of Sociology, 43 (1937), 404-413.

_____, Men and Their Work, New York: Free Press, 1958.

_____, "Social Change and Status Protest: An Essay on the Marginal Man," Phylon, 10 (1949), 58-65.

Huxley, Aldous, Brave New World, New York: Harpers, 1932.

Inkles, Alex, "Social Structure and Socialization," In Goslin, David A., (ed.), Handbook of Socialization Theory and Research, Chicago: Rand McNally College Publishing Co., 1973:615-632.

Jackson, J., "Reference Group Processes in a Formal Organization," In Cartwright, C. and Zander, A., (eds.), Group Dynamics: Research and Theory, New York: Harper & Row, 1960.

James, William, Principles of Psychology, 2 Vols., New York: Henry Holt, 1890 or Cleveland: World Publishing Co., 1948.

Jones, Delmos J., "Toward a Native Anthropology," Human Organization, 29, 4 (Winter 1970), 251-259.

Kahn, R.L., Wolfe, D.M., Quinn, R.P., and Snock, J.D., Organizational Stress: Studies in Role Conflict and Ambiguity, New York: John Wiley, 1964.

Kanter, Rosabeth Moss, Men and Women of the Corporation, New York: Basic Books, Inc., 1977.

Kardiner, A., The Individual and His Society, New York: Columbia University Press, 1939.

Katz, Daniel and Robert L. Kahn, The Social Psychology of Organizations, New York: John Wiley and Sons, Inc., 1966, 171-198.

Katz, E. and Eisenstadt, S.N., "Some Sociological Observations on the Response of Israeli Organizations to New Immigrants," Administrative Science Quarterly, 5 (1960), 113-133.

Kelley, H., "Salience of Membership and Resistance to Change of Group-Anchored Attitudes," Human Relations, 8, 3 (1955), 275-289.

Kerckhoff, A.C., and McCormick, T.C, "Marginal Status and Marginal Personality," Social Forces, 34 (1955), 48-55.

Kluckhohn, C., "Theoretical Bases for an Empirical Method of Studying the Acquisition of Culture by Individuals," Man, 39 (1939), 98-103. Reprinted in Kluckhohn, C., Culture and Behavior, New York: The Free Press of Glencoe, 1962.

Knezevitch, Stephen J., Administration of Public Education, New York: Harper and Row, Publishers, 3rd Edition, 1975.

Knabe, D., "Consistency and Community," Social Forces, 51 (1972), 23-33.

Kobayashe, K. Jessie, A Comparison of Organizational Climate of Schools Administered by Female and Male Elementary School Principals, Dissertation Abstract, University of the Pacific, 1974, 129-a - 130-a.

Kochan, Thomas A., Schmidt, Stuart M. and De Cotiis, Thomas A., "Superior-Subordinate Relations: Leadership and Headship," Human Relations, 28, 3 (1975), 279-294.

Komarovsky, M., "Functional Analysis of Sex Roles," American Sociological Review, 15 (1950), 508-516.

Kuhn, Manford, "Major Trends in Symbolic Interaction Theory in the Past Twenty-five Years," Sociological Quarterly, 5 (Winter, 1969), 61-84.

LaPiere, R., A Theory of Social Control, New York: McGraw-Hill Book Co., Inc., 1954.

Lennard, H.K., and Bernstein, A., The Anatomy of Psychotherapy, New York: Columbia University Press, 1960.

Leopold, Edith A., "Community Representation: A Study of Role Perceptions and Behavior," Human Relations, 26, 6 (1973), 695-713.

LeVine, Robert A., "Culture, Personality and Socialization: An Evolutionary View," In Goslin, David A., (ed.), Handbook of Socialization Theory and Research, Chicago: Rand McNally College Publishing Co., 1973: 503-542.

Levinson, D., "Role, Personality and Social Structure in the Organizational Setting," Journal of Abnormal and Social Psychology, 58 (1959), 170-180.

Lewin, K., A Dynamic Theory of Personality: Selected Papers, New York: McGraw-Hill Book Co., 1935.

Lewis, Diana, "Anthropology and Colonialism, "Current Anthropology, 14, 5 (December, 1973), 581-602.

Lewis, Lionel S., Scaling the Ivory Tower: Merit and Its Limits in Academic Careers, Baltimore: Johns Hopkins Press, 1975.

Linton, Ralph, The Study of Man: An Introduction, New York: Appleton-Century-Crofts, 1936.

Longstreth, Catherine Archibald, An Analysis of the Perceptions of the Leadership Behavior of Male and Female Secondary School Principals in Florida, Dissertation Abstract, University of Miami, 1973, 2224-a - 2225-a.

Lortie, Dan C., "The Balance of Control and Automomy in Elementary School Teaching," In Etzioni, A., (ed.), The Semi-professions and Their Organization, New York: Free Press, 1969.

Lortie, Dan C., Schoolteacher: A Sociological Study, Chicago: The University of Chicago, 1975.

Lumpkin, Katherine, The Family: A Study of Member Roles, Chapel Hill: The University of North Carolina, 1933.

Lynd, R.S. and Lynd, Helen M., Middletown: A Study in Contemporary American Culture, New York: Harcourt, Brace, 1929.

Malinowsky, Bronislaw, Argonauts of the Western Pacific, London: Routledge & Kegaan Paul, 1922.

Malinowsky, Bronislaw, Sex and Repression in Savage Society, New York: Humanities Press, 1927 or Meridian Books Edition, World Publishing, 1955.

March, James G. and Simon, H.A., Organizations, New York: Wiley, 1958.

Marshall, Catherine, The Career Socializaton of Women in School Administration, Unpublished Dissertation, University of California, Santa Barbara, 1979.

Mascaro, Francis, C., The Early on the Job Socialization of First-year Elementary School Principals, Unpublished doctoral dissertation, University of California, Riverside, 1973.

Mason, Ward, The Beginning Teacher, Washington, D.C.: U.S. Government Printing Office, 1961.

Mauss, Marcel, The Gift: Forms and Functions in Archaic Societies, New York: W. W. Norton, 1967, 40.

McCabe, Dennis P., Bureaucratic Role and Socialization: A Replication of Bridges' Study on the Elementary Principal, Unpublished doctoral dissertation, University of New Mexico, 1972.

McDougall, W., An Introduction to Social Psychology, Boston: Luce, 1908.

McGivney, Joseph H., and Haught, James, "The Politics of Education: A View from the Perspective of the Central Office Staff," Educational Administration Quarterly, 8, 3 (Autumn, 1972), 18–38.

Mead, George Herbert, Mind, Self and Society, Chicago: University of Chicago Press, 1934.

Mead, Margaret, Coming of Age in Samoa, New York: William Morrow & Co., 1928.

_____, "Socialization and Enculturation," Current Anthropology, 4 (1963), 184–187.

Merton, R. K., "The Role-set: Problems in Sociological Theory," British Journal of Sociology, 8 (1957), 106–120.

_____, "The Search for Professional Status: Sources, Costs, and Consequences," American Journal of Nursing, 70 (May 1960), 662–664.

_____, Social Structure and Anomie,"American Sociological Review, 3 (October, 1938), 677–682.

_____, Social Theory and Social Structure, (Revised edition), Glencoe: Free Press, 1957.

Meskin, Joan D., "Women as Principals: Their Performance as Educational Administrators," In Erickson, Donald A., and Reller, Theodore L, (eds.) The Principal in Metropolitan Schools, Berkeley, California: McCutchan, 1978.

Miller, D., "The Study of Social Relationships: Situation, Identity and Social Interaction," In Kock, S. (ed.), Psychology: A Study of a Science, New York: McGraw-Hill, 1963:639–737.

Mills, C. Wright, The Power Elite, New York: Oxford University Press, 1956.

_____, The Sociological Imagination, London: Oxford, 1959.

Minkler, Meredith, and Biller, Robert P., "Role Shock: A Tool for Conceptualizing Stresses Accompanying Disruptive Role Transitions," Human Relations, 32, 2 (1979), 125-140.

Moore, Wilbert E., "Occupational Socialization," In Goslin, David A., (ed.) Handbook of Socialization Theory and Research, Chicago: Rand McNally, 1973:861-884.

Moreno, Jacob, "Who Shall Survive?" Nervous and Mental Disease Publication, Washington, D.C., 1936; Revised edition, New York: Beacon House, 1953.

Murphy, G., Murphy, Lois B., and Newcomb, T., Experimental Social Psychology: An Interpretation of Research on the Socialization of the Individual, 2nd ed., New York: Harper, 1937.

Murray, Henry L, Explorations in Personality, New York: Oxford University Press, 1938.

Mussen, P.H., Conger, J.J. and Kagan, J., Child Development and Personality, 2nd ed,. New York: Harper & Row, 1963:409.

Nadel, Siegfried Frederick, The Theory of Social Structure, London: Cohen & West, 1957.

Naegele, K., Editorial Forward to Section C: "The Modes of the Institutionalization of Action," In Parsons, T., Shils, E., Naegele, K., and Pitts, J. R. (eds.), Theories of Society: Foundations of Modern Sociological Theory, Vol. 1, Glencoe: Free Press, 1961.

National Council of Administrative Women in Education (NCAWE), Wanted: More Women - Where are the Women Superintendents? Arlington, Va.: NCAWE, 1973.

National Education Association (NEA), 25th Biennial Salary Survey of Public School Professional Personnel, Research Report 1971-R5 (Washington D.C.: Research Division, NEA, 1971).

National Education Association, (NEA), 26th Biennial Salary Survey of Public School Professional Personnel, Research Report 1973-R5 (Washington, D. C.: Research Division, NEA, 1973).

National Education Association (NEA), The Elementary Principal in 1968 (Washington, D.C.: Department of Elementary School Principals, NEA, 1968).

Newcomb, T. M., The Acquaintance Process, New York: Holt, Rinehart & Winston, 1961.

Nixon, Mary and Gue, L.R., "Professional Role Orientation of Women Administrators and Women Teachers," The Canadian Administrator, 15, 2 (November, 1975), 1-4.

Oberg, K., Consultation in the Brazil-United States Cooperative Health Program, 1945-1955, Rio De Janeiro: U. S. Operations Mission to Brazil, Institute of Inter-American Affairs, 1955.

Ogburn, W.F. and Nimhoff, M.F., Sociology, Boston: Houghton Mifflin Co., 1940.

Ortiz, Flora Ida, The Process of Professional Incorporation, Unpublished doctoral dissertation, University of New Mexico, 1972.

_____, "Socialization Processes of Central Office Personnel," Paper presented at the American Educational Research Association Convention, San Francisco, California, 1979.

_____, and Venegas, Yolanda, "Chicana (Female) School Administrators," Emergent Leadership, 2, 2 (Spring, 1978), 55-59.

Orwell, George, 1984: A Novel, New York: Brace & Co., 1949.

Paloma, Margaret M. and Garland, T. Neal, "The Married Professional Woman: A Study in the Tolerance of Domestication," Journal of Marriage and the Family, 33, 3 (August 1971), 531-540.

Park, R.E., Race and Culture, Glencoe, Ill.: The Free Press, 1950.

Park, R.E., "Symbiosis and Socialization: A Frame of Reference for the Study of Society," American Journal of Sociolgy, 45 (1939), 1-25.

Parsons, Talcott, The Social System, New York: Free Press, 1951.

Pfeffer, Jeffrey, and Salancik, Gerald R., "Determinants of Supervisory Behavior; A Role Set Analysis," Human Relations, 28, 2 (1975), 139-154.

Pittenger, Benjamin F., Local Public School Administration, New York: McGraw-Hill Book Co., Inc., 1951, 51-52.

Presthus, Robert, The Organizational Society, New York: Alfred A. Knopf, Inc., 1962.

Rabinowitz, L., Kelly, H.H., and Rosenblatt, R.M., "Effects of Different Types of Interdependence and Response Conditions in the Minimal Social Situation," Journal of Experimental Social Psychology, 2 (1966), 169-197.

Radcliffe-Brown, A.R., Structure and Functions in Primitive Society, New York: The Free Press, 1965, 90-91.

Ravitch, Diane, The Great School Wars of New York City, 1805-1973: A History of the Public Schools as Battlefield of Social Change, New York: Basic Books, Inc., 1974.

Reed, Donald B., A Study of the Collaborative Work of Specialists and Teachers in Schools, Unpublished doctoral dissertation, University of California, Riverside, 1980.

Richardson, A., "The Assimilation of British Immigrants in a Western Australian Community: A Psychological Study," R.E.M.P. Bulletin, Double Issue, 9 (1961), 1-71.

_____, "A Theory and A Method for the Psychological Study of Assimilation," International Migration Review, 2 (1967), 3-30.

Riesman, David; Glazer, Nathan; Denny, Reuel, The Lonely Crowd: A Study of the Changing American Character, New Haven, Conn.: Yale University Press, 1961.

Roethlisberger, F. and W. Dickson, Management and the Worker, Cambridge, Mass.: Harvard University Press, 1939.

Rodgers, David, 110 Livingston Street: Politics and Bureaucracy in the New York City Schools, New York; Random House, 1968.

Rommetweit, R., Social Norms and Roles, Minneapolis: University of Minnesota Press, 1955.

Rose, A.M., Human Behavior and Social Processes: An Interactionist Approach, Boston: Houghton-Mifflin Co., 1962.

Ross, E.A., "Social Control," American Journal of Sociology, 1 (1896), 513-535.

_____, Social Psychology, New York: The Macmillan Co., 1908.

Saltonstall, R., Human Relations in Administration, New York: McGraw-Hill Book Co., Inc., 1959.

Sampson, E.E., "Status Congruence and Cognitive Consistency," Sociometry, 26 (1963), 146-162.

Sapir, E., "The Unconscious Patterning of Behavior in Society," In Mandeblaum, D. G. (ed.), Edward Sapir: Selected Writings in Language, Culture and Personality, Berkeley: University of California Press, 1949:544-559.

Sarbin, T.R., "Role Theory," In Lindzey, G., (ed.), Handbook of Social Psychology, Vol. 1, Cambridge, Mass.: Addison-Wesley Publishing Co., 1954: 223-258.

Sargent, Stephen Stansfeld, Social Psychology: An Integrative Interpretation, New York: Ronald Press Co., 1950.

Schein, E.H., Coercive Persuasion, New York: Norton, 1961.

_____, "Organizational Socialization and the Profession of Management," Industrial Management Review, 9 (1968), 1-15.

_____, "The Individual, the Organization, and the Career: A Conceptual Scheme," The Journal of Applied Behavioral Science, 7, 4 (1971), 401-426.

Scriven, Alvenia L. and Nunnery, Michael Y., "Women Central Office Administrators in Large Urban Districts: Characteristics and Perceptions, "Educational Horizons, 52, 3 (Spring, 1975), 138-142.

Seeman, M., Social Status and Leadership: The Case of the School Executive, Columbus, Ohio: Ohio State University, Bureau of Educational Research, 1960.

Shaw, C. R., The Jack-Roller: A Delinquent Boy's Own Story, Chicago: University of Chicago Press, 1930.

Sherif, M., "The Concept of Reference Groups in Human Relations," In Sherif, M. and Wilson, M., (eds.), Group Relations at the Crossroads, New York: Harper and Brothers, 1953.

Shibutani, T., "Reference Groups and Social Control," In Rose, A., (ed.), Human Behavior and Social Processes, Boston: Houghton-Mifflin Co., 1962.

Shils, Edward, "The Calling of Sociology," In Parsons, T., Shils, E., Naegele, K., and Pitts, J. R., (eds.), Theories of Society: Foundations of Modern Sociological Theory, Vol. 1, Glencoe: Free Press, 1961.

Simmel, G., "The Problem of Sociology," Annal of the American Academy of Political and Social Science, 6 (1895), 412-423.

Snow, R. J. and Edward S. Hickox, "National Study of School Superintendents," 1967. Cited in Carlson, R. O., School Superintendents: Careers and Performance, Columbus, Ohio: Merrill, 1972.

Spence, Betty A., "Sex of Teachers as a Factor in Their Perception of Selected Leadership Characteristics of Male and Female Elementary School Principals," Dissertation Abstract, Purdue University, 1971: 2985-a.

Spradley, James P. and Brenda J. Mann, The Cocktail Waitress, New York: John Wiley and Sons, Inc., 1975.

Starr, Paul D., "Marginality, Role Conflict and Status Inconsistency as Forms of Stressful Interaction," Human Relations, 30, 10 (1977), 949-961.

Stogdill, R., Individual Behavior and Group Achievement, New York: Oxford University Press, 1959.

Stonequist, E. V., The Marginal Man, New York: Scribner's, 1937.

Sullivan, H. S., Conceptions of Modern Psychiatry, 2nd ed., New York: W. W. Norton & Co., 1953.

Sutherland, R. L. and Woodward, J., Introductory Sociology, New York: J. B. Lippincott Co., 1937.

Sutton, F. X., Harris, S. E., Kaysen, C., and Tobin, J., The American Business Creed, Cambridge: Harvard University Press, 1956.

Tannenbaum, A., "Control in Organizations: Individual Adjustment and Organizational Performance," Administrative Science Quarterly, 7 (1962), 236-257.

Thomas, W. I.,"The Persistence of Primary-Group Norms in Present-day Society and Their Influence in our Educational System," In Jennings, H. S., Watson, John B., and Meyer, Adolf, Suggestions of Modern Science Concerning Education, New York: The Macmillan Co., 1917, 167-187.

Thomas, W. I. and Zanaiecki, F., The Polish Peasant in Europe and America, 4 Vols., Boston: Richard C. Badger, 1918-20 or New York: Dover Pub., 1958.

Thompson, James D., Organizations in Action, New York: McGraw-Hill, 1967.

Torens, Nina, "The Bus Driver: A Study in Role Analysis," Human Relations, 26, 1 (1973), 101-112.

Turner, Barbara F. and McCaffey, Joanne Hammar, "Socialization and Career Orientation Among Black and White College Women," Journal of Vocational Behavior, 5 (1974), 307-319.

Turner, Jonathan H., The Structure of Sociological Theory, Homewood, Ill.: The Dorsey Press, 1978.

Turner, R. H.,"Sponsored and Contest Mobility and the School System," American Sociological Review, 25 (1960), 855-867.

U. S. Commission on Civil Rights, Mexican-American Education Study, Ethnic Isolation of Mexican-Americans in the Public Schools of the Southwest, Report 1, Washington, D. C.: U. S. Commission on Civil Rights, April, 1971.

Valverde, Leonard A., Succession Socialization: Its Influences on School Administration Candidates and Its Implication to the Exclusion of Minorities From Administration, Washington, D. C.: National Institute of Education, Project 3-0813, 1974.

Venegas, Yolanda, Chicanas in Educational Administration: A Study of Public School Administrators in the Greater Los Angeles Metropolitan Area, Unpublished doctoral dissertation, Brigham Young University, Salt Lake City, Utah, 1977.

Vidich, Arthur J., and Bensman, Joseph, Small Town in Mass Society, Garden City, New York: Doubleday & Co., 1960.

Waller, Willard, Sociology of Teaching, New York: Wiley, 1933.

Warner, W. L., Personal Communication with Clausen, 1969.

Weber, Max, From Max Weber: Essays in Sociology, Translated and Edited by H. H. Gerth and C. Wright Mills, New York: Oxford University Press, 1969 Reprint, 196-244.

Weber, M., The Theory of Social and Economic Organization, Translated by A. M. Henderson and T. Parsons, (eds.), Glencoe: Free Press, 1947.

Weick, Karl E., The Scoial Psychology of Organizing, Reading, Mass.: Addison-Wesley, 1969.

White, Winston, Beyond Conformity, New York: Free Press of Glencoe, 1961.

176   CAREER PATTERNS IN EDUCATION

Whiting, J. W. M., Becoming a Kwoma: Teaching and Learning in a New Guinea Tribe, New Haven, Conn.: Yale University Press, 1941.

Whiting, J.W.M., and Child, J.R., Child Training and Personality. New Haven, Conn.: Yale University Press, 1953.

Whyte, William H., The Organization Man, New York: Doubleday and Co., Inc., 1956.

Wiggins, Tom W., "Why Our Urban Schools are Leaderless," Education and Urban Society, 2 (1970), 169-178.

Wiley, Bennie Lee, Jr., Variables That Affect Administrative Behavior, Dissertation Abstract, University of Miami, 1973, 2252-a - 2253-a.

Wolcott, Harry F., The Man in the Principal's Office: An Ethnography, New York: Holt, Rinehart and Winston, Inc., 1973.

Wray, D. E., "The Marginal Man of Industry: The Foreman," American Journal of Sociology, 14 (1949), 298-301.

Young, Donald B., "The Socialization of American Minority Peoples," In Goslin, David A., (ed.), Handbook of Socialization Theory and Research, Chicago: Rand McNally, 1973, 1103-1140.

Young, K., Social Psychology, New York: Alfred A. Knopf, 1930.

NAME INDEX

SUBJECT INDEX

  group, 143, 144
  manipulated, 124, 125
  outward, 138
  supervisor, 133
Constraints, 132, 133
Consultant, 18, 28
Containing community conflict, 20
Content area specialization, 13
Control, 21, 22
  loss of, 33
Convergence, 145
Coordinators, 13, 20, 31, 32
Coping mechanisms, 137, 138
Cultural forms, 125
Culture, 123
  shock, 143
  transmission of, 125

Debureaucratization, 139
Decision-makers, 13, 72, 131
  superintendents, 13
  supervisors, 131
  women, 73
Defeminized behavior, 134
Delinquency, 121
Demotion, 9, 29
  minority principals, 109–110
Departing from teaching, 9
Dependence, 139
Deposits of opportunity, 3
Deposits of power, 3
Director, 13, 19, 29
  assistant, 19, 29
  elementary education, 30
  influence, 97, 99
  special projects, 98, 99
Discipline, 128
Distance from: core, 23
  superintendent, 23
District information, 21, 24
District meetings, 13, 14
  functions of, 16
Division of labor, 52
Domestication of women, 72
Double consciousness, 132

Education, 125
Education of the child, 125
Educational administration, 1
Elementary principals, 2, 3, 11–16, 25, 35, 79, 80, 81, 111–113
  Hispanic female, 113–117
  interpersonal relationships, 14
  movement, 15, 16
  opportunity, 16
  perceptions towards superintendent, 13
  permanency, 11, 36
  responsibility, 15
  school days, 16

  tasks, 15
  women, 69–72
Elementary school, 11
  administrative units, 12
  males in, 9
Entry into, 25–27
  level, 7
Ethnic origin, 3
Evaluation process, 35
  specialists, 62
Exclusion of minority principals, 105–108
Expectations, 130
  externally imposed, 137, 138
  formalized, 140
  Hispanic female administrator, 110–115
  minorities, 92–94, 104
  peer, 132, 134
  script, 129
  structurally imposed, 137, 138
  subordinate, 133, 134
  women, 58
Experience, 3, 27, 149
  extraordinary, 30
  Hispanic female, 111, 112–115
  senior high school principal, 11

Female administrator relationships, 78, 80
Focal persons, 132, 133
Formal procedures, 35
Functions of meetings, 16
  special projects, 99

GASing, 31–33, 61, 70
Governance, 17

Hierarchical level, 3
Hierarchical placement, 19
  vice-principal, 8
Hierarchical position of: specialists, 62
  supervisors, 67
Hierarchy, 3, 8, 19, 62, 67, 94, 95, 103, 104
  principal, 11
  minority principal, 105, 106
  special projects, 96
High school, 11–16, 24
High school principal, 13, 36, 37
  aspirations, 14
  interpersonal relationships, 16
  women, 69
Hiring practices: Hispanic female, 110–115
  minorities, 90–92
Humor, 35, 36

Identification, 126
  change, 136, 137
  crisis, 145, 146
  group, 144
  stage, 145
  subidentity, 137